EAT

Sleep

seek

STRIDE

AN AUTOBIOGRAPHICAL WELLNESS GUIDE

THEODORA WILNER

BALBOA.
PRESS

A DIVISION OF HAY HOUSE

Balboa Press books may be ordered through booksellers or by contacting:

Balboa Press
A Division of Hay House
1663 Liberty Drive
Bloomington, IN 47403
www.balboapress.com
1 (877) 407-4847

Print information available on the last page.

ISBN: 978-1-5043-4807-2 (sc)
ISBN: 978-1-5043-4808-9 (e)

Library of Congress Control Number: 2016901182

Balboa Press rev. date: 02/22/2016

This book is dedicated to:

The memory of my friend,
Jane Carney

The mindfulness of my husband,
Bruce

The magic of my children,
Autumn & Aurora

An excerpt from

"The Paradox of Our Time…"

…Is that we have taller buildings but shorter tempers, wider freeways, but narrower viewpoints…We have more degrees but less sense, more knowledge, but less judgment, more experts, yet more problems, more medicine, but less wellness.

We drink too much, smoke too much, spend too recklessly, laugh too little, drive too fast, get too angry, stay up too late, get up too tired, read too little, watch TV too much, and pray too seldom…

George Carlin, written after 9/11

CONTENTS

- Medicinal effects of various foods
- Maintaining control when dining out with friends
- Politely declining desserts without feeling guilty
- Evidence-based research on wellness
- Healing lungs after years of smoking
- Why do we need Vitamin D?
- Non-Medical ways to reduce high blood pressure
- Avoiding excessive sun exposure
- Tools for controlling moods
- Effects of EMR
- Coffee: What's the truth?
- More on aging
- Wash Your Hands
- How little can I do and give up and still be healthy?

PREFACE AND ACKNOWLEDGMENTS

Eat, Sleep, Seek, and Stride: An Autobiographical Wellness Guide is based on a keynote address I delivered at a Women's Health Conference in Sacramento in May 2015, entitled *Eat Fat, Seek the Dark, and Stride.*

I chose this provocative title because I wanted to get the audience's attention and to reverse their assumptions. I was *not* inviting them to chug a gallon of cooking oil or join Darth Vader on the Dark Side. Rather, I was asking them — as I ask you— to look at Wellness from a different perspective. I want to shake up your paradigms and get you to look at food, exercise, and your place in the world with fresh eyes. It is time for us — for a whole new generation —to become re-focused and open to a new dialog about food, exercise, preserving our earth, and what makes living worthwhile. In so doing, you will become healthier and happier.

I shortened the title for this book from the original speech, because a friend told me she would never buy a book that told her to eat fat. She also said that "seeking the dark" sounded "depressing and scary, like a cold dark cave with spider webs and bats and slick moss on the rocks and hidden dragons."

About 10,000 words into the book, I was getting bored with myself. The manuscript was sounding like one of those grocery store checkout line magazine articles that promises you can "Lose 10 pounds in 10 days," or "Get rid of Stress *Forever*" or "Age without wrinkles." I was regurgitating everything I had ever learned, but saying very little about what I have come to know.

So I started getting a little more personal. Before I knew it, I was telling you everything about why I have pursued wellness: my overeating, my troubling childhood, my insomnia, my arthritis, my scoliosis, my herniated disk, and my belief system.

Two "interventions" have been the most influential in shaping my body, mind, and spirit. This book tells you about both of these avenues to freedom.

First, is my 35-year involvement in the wellness movement. Through wellness, I have learned methods and techniques for achieving optimal health. I have learned that I know best what is best for me. I have learned that natural healing practices, not always offered by mainstream medical practice, can be just as effective for me, with fewer side effects. I have come to know that taking care of myself and the world around me, go hand in hand. Mostly I have learned that the greatest truths are the simplest.

Second, is my 40-year practice of YOGA. YOGA is an ancient spiritual practice that invites us to become self-realized, to connect with our inner source, to find truth, peace, and wisdom. YOGA, a Sanskrit word, is derived from the same root word as "Yoke"; it is about *yoking* your everyday self to your higher self. When I am able to come from that place, my life is filled with joy, compassion, and serenity. If I come off as a YOGA zealot, it is because I am.

You do not need to practice YOGA to be whole, happy, and free. But you must find a passion for *something* with similar benefits that works for you.

When I was a drug rehabilitation counselor, back in the 80s, I stumbled on a book called *Positive Addiction* (by William Glasser, M.D., 1985.) I subscribe to Dr. Glasser's thesis that we all have addictive tendencies. The best way to counter *negative* addictions (e.g., food, TV, substances) is to find a *positive* addiction, something you love to do (e.g., running, dancing, singing).

I have come to believe that you must find activities that make you healthy and happy before you can release your negative patterns. My hope is that this book will prompt you to do just that.

I could not have written this book without the input and support of many people. Many thanks to:

> My parents, for giving me the strength and tenacity to persevere.

> Dulce Murphy and Jerry Brown for creating the California Governor's Council on Wellness and Physical Fitness and for hiring me to run it.

> My husband, Bruce, for sticking with me through thick and thin.

My daughters, Autumn and Aurora, for keeping me on my toes and teaching me what is really important in life.

Mackenzie Cecchi, for her cover design and graphic brilliance.

My editor, Alice Schilla, for hours of reading and re-reading this text, making substantive recommendations as well as correcting the small stuff.

My neighbor, Nancy Lawrence, for offering me a different perspective and challenging me to be clear.

The Institute for Integrative Nutrition® for enhancing my wellness education and inspiring me to finish this book.

The hundreds of yoga students I have taught for the past 20 years, who have given me a reason for being, and

Ananda, for keeping me spiritually-grounded.

HOW TO USE THIS BOOK

"You may not be responsible for being down, but
you must be responsible for getting up."
Jesse Jackson

The main purpose of this book is to motivate change.

Sometimes all it takes is the acquisition of knowledge to become empowered. Other times, it takes an active intervention. This book contains interactive exercises to enliven your experience. If you are interested in assessing, addressing, and attacking your health limitations, you will want to do these exercises!

By practicing the tenets of wellness, you will have more energy and joy, your life will become easier, and you will enjoy a quality drug-free, pain-free life till the end of your days.

If you are not able to work through this book on your own, find a friend, or bring a few friends together. "In union there is strength." *(Aesop)*

There may come a point when you want to reach out to me. If so, here's my e-mail address: theodora@wilnwerweb.com.

INTRODUCTION

What is Wellness?

"Your own best doctor resides within."
Albert Schweitzer

The basic tenets of a wellness practice are not complicated. When you practice wellness, you:

- Eat whole foods (EAT)
- Sleep well (SLEEP)
- Build positive relationships (SEEK)
- Find spirit or purpose and meaning (SEEK)
- Live joyfully (SEEK)
- Protect your environment (EAT, SEEK)
- Move your body (STRIDE)
- Manage stress and develop resilience (take things in STRIDE)
- Experience your highest potential (hit your STRIDE)

In 1981, I was appointed by then Governor Brown as the Executive Director of the California Governor's Council on Wellness and Physical Fitness. It was the first statewide commission dedicated to the promotion of health.

The Wellness Council organized its projects and plans around the following "planks" of wellness:

- Self-responsibility
- Nutritional awareness
- Stress management
- Physical fitness, and
- Environmental sensitivity

We borrowed these five dimensions of wellness from Don Ardell's groundbreaking book: *High Level Wellness: An Alternative to Doctors, Drugs, and Disease* (Rodale Press, 1977).

John W. Travis, MD, another early wellness pioneer, gave up the practice of sick care to open the first wellness center in the U.S. in 1975. He is said to have launched the term "Wellness" into the public eye. Travis's "Wellness Inventory" remains one of the best and most comprehensive wellness assessments in the market and is accessed as the centerpiece of a whole person wellbeing program at www.wellpeople.com.

Wellness is a simple, obvious concept, but the term was belittled when it was first introduced as a touchy-feely, radical, far- out concept that Governor "Moonbeam" tried to legitimize. Fortunately, the radicalism of the 80s has become the common sense of today. In his return to the Governorship of California, Jerry Brown is respected as a strong, pragmatic leader.

Wellness is now mainstream and is seen as a valid preventative to many causes of death and disability. Unfortunately, it is *not* universally practiced.

This book invites you to challenge your resistance to wellness practice as I have challenged my own resistance.

I've been fat most of my life. I feel like I've endured every diet known to mankind: Atkins, Pritikin, Diet Center, Grapefruit, Slimfast, South Beach, Starvation, Weight Watchers, and the Zone, to name a few. I've taken Dexamyl (an early amphetamine), "Phen-Fen," (a lethal drug combination that has since been banned), B12 injections, and countless other supplements and alleged miracle potions of questionable origin. I've gone to doctors where I've been injected with shots of unknown value. One doctor molested me during a pre-op physical.

Five years ago, I worked with a nutritionist who assisted me in losing 20 pounds that I have kept off. I was comforted by her humanity and inspired by her knowledge – so much so that I went on to secure a health coaching certification through the *Institute for Integrative Nutrition*®. I am now a certified health coach and a public speaker. I feel much better about myself.

I am not, however, thin. I still carry an extra 12 pounds. I struggle daily with a "fat head" and persistent habits that are not always in my best interest. Often, I feel I am not credible enough to stand in front of audiences or to support clients. Who am I to offer support when I haven't fully mastered the clean eating component of a complete wellness practice?

It turns out that most of us are not perfect. It's about progress, not perfection. We are all working on something. We all have our battles. My food addiction has plagued me, but also keeps me real and compassionate and devoted to the cause of wellness as a practice worth pursuing and promoting. I've come a long way.

One thing I've learned, which is projected throughout this book, is that no one can tell someone else how to eat, exercise, and live. It is something you have to figure out for yourself. What I can and do offer in this book is information and knowledge that you can use to your own advantage. It is likely that you know much of what I will be telling you. My hope it that either I will transmit the information in a new way that inspires you to make changes, or you are simply at a point of readiness to hear it.

I hope the knowledge I have gained in my life, and the candid revelation of my personal struggle with food and other challenges, will inspire you to make some of the changes necessary to feel better and make your life easier.

The Only Certain Thing in Life is Change

"Be the change you wish to see in the world"

Mahatma Gandhi

Sometimes, solutions to health problems are so simple that people don't believe in them. Most patients prefer to seek treatment outside themselves for vague health complaints. Physicians become Gods of problem solving, and most patients are disappointed if they leave their doctor's office without a pharmaceutical prescription.

While the *concept* of wellness is simple, a wellness *practice* is not always easy. It requires a modification of existing habits and patterns. It requires change.

We must first acknowledge that we are always changing. Our bodies change over time. Our activity levels change. Our environment changes. Our hormones change. Our preferences change. Our partners change. We change with the seasons. We are changed by the weather. We are changed by the pollution in our air and water. We are changed by the pesticides on our foods and by the genetic modification of our foods.

If we wish to be evolved human beings, our thoughts and opinions must also change. We must be open-minded and resilient.

One of my favorite stories on this theme is about a young woman who takes over the hosting of Thanksgiving from her grandmother.

The whole family is gathered in the kitchen when Granddaughter pulls a magnificent, browned turkey out of the oven.

"Why is your turkey split in half?" Grandma asks.

*"Of course it's cut in half. That's the way **you** did it, Grandma."*

"Honey, I cut the turkey in half because the whole turkey would not fit into my oven."

We've listened to our parents who have listened to their parents, and we have integrated ideas and traditions from our old teachers, friends, and peers that may no longer be valid or serve us. We are an amalgam of people and times past. It is time to move on.

We need to be resilient when it comes to taking care of our health. We need to be attentive to our own body, educated to changing trends, and mindful of our true needs. We also need to see our health in the context of the health of the planet. How we change must consider the offerings and limitations of our earth.

People, Pyramids, and Policies

I've identified three main reasons for the resistance to wellness. I call these influences the "Three Ps": People, Pyramids, and Policies.

Most of this book addresses the "People" part of the equation. We will look at the impediments to our personal mastery of wellness practices and what we can do to overcome them.

We are living in ways that assault our essential nature and Mother Nature. We are tired, overworked, and under-loved. We are not being nourished on a primary level, and so we have become lethargic and sedentary or have turned to food, drink, and electronic devices to satisfy our unmet desires.

The food pyramid has provided nationally sanctioned dietary guidelines for two generations. In *Eat, Sleep, Seek & Stride,* you will learn that these guidelines were based on unsubstantiated science and special interests. In fact, the original food pyramid may have inadvertently triggered the obesity epidemic and agricultural priorities that are not in our best interest.

Policies have determined what and how farmers grow, and what foods are most and least available to the American people. Policies have supported a food manufacturing industry that has addicted us to high fructose corn syrup and hydrogenated fats. If, like me, you are a yo-yo dieter who has reverted to rich, sugary foods time and time again, you will be heartened to know that this is not your fault. Food scientists have created extremely flavorful, highly-addictive foods that have hijacked our taste buds into preferring these artificial and addictive victuals.

Simultaneously, we are witnessing the proliferation of crops that are bred for portability, size, and disease resistance instead of flavor. This sometimes leaves them tasteless.

"The food we should be eating is getting more bland and the food we should not be eating is getting more flavorful!" says

Mark Schatzker author of *The Dorito Effect; the Surprising new truth about Food and Flavor.*

There is a way out of this cycle. This book will show you that way.

Environmental Sensitivity

"I am he as you are he as you are me and we are all together…"
From "I am the Walrus" by the Beatles

"Protecting the earth" and "environmental sensitivity" are important components of wellness that are not always mentioned or included in a wellness program or practice. Indeed, my editor questioned my recommendations to eat locally-grown produce and humanely-raised animals. "These are important ethical issues," she said, "but how do they relate to Wellness?"

Wellness presupposes a lifestyle in which you are living in balance with yourself, with other people, and with the land around you. A well body and mind will not thrive in a polluted earth or a cruel and inhumane society. The more you practice the ways of wellness, the more you wake up to the need for kind and fair treatment of all beings.

"Live lightly on the earth. Make do with less, avoid disposable and processed products. Recycle, cut back on convenience items, insulate your home, eat lower on the food chain, compost your organic wastes, and use energy from the sun."
From High Level Wellness by Don Ardell, 1977

PART I

EAT

This section introduces the concept of "Primary Foods." Nourishment of the mind, body, and spirit is of primary importance; the food on your plate is secondary to this. Food can fill you, but it cannot fulfill you.

You can evaluate your "Primary Foods" by completing the Interactive Wellness Wheel. This is your first exercise. Do not skip this step. It sets the tone for the whole book.

Although this section offers many dietary theories, they are simply informational. It is important for you to know that fat is not the enemy and the outdated food pyramid is not your friend.

How do you decide what foods are best for you, when bombarded by conflicting dietary theories? The answer is found in a one-sentence dietary guideline, the "secret you already know."

A key goal of this section is to accept your uniqueness and to develop your own food plan. You'll be given a template for creating a personalized food pyramid. You will also be given some insight on cravings along with seven tips for overcoming them.

Finally, healthy eating cannot be achieved without a healthy earth. Environmental sensitivity is intrinsic to wellness.

Chapter 1

PRIMARY FOODS

Joshua Rosenthal, founder of the Institute for Integrative Nutrition® (my nutrition school) created this concept. "Primary" foods include supportive relationships, consistent physical activity, sleeping well, happiness, learning, creativity, and finding meaning, to name a few. Primary foods are nourishing. The food you put in your mouth is secondary to these attributes of a healthy life.

This is really the crux of the food story. It makes no sense to diet or clean up our food act before looking at how our life is going. We must be nourished by what we do, by where we work and live, by how we spend our time, and by the people with whom we spend our time. Absent these, we become vulnerable to the addictive and isolating comforts of food, drink, and other unhealthy substances.

One of the first food authors to make this point was Geneen Roth. *When Food is Love, Breaking Free from Emotional Eating,* and *Feeding the Hungry Heart* were breakthrough books for a generation of overeaters such as myself who blamed themselves for losing and gaining the same 40 pounds over and over again.

"For every diet," she told us, "there is an equal and opposite binge."

Geneen Roth revolutionized the food movement and gave hope to millions who were filled with shame and self-flagellation for their inappropriate eating habits. She asked us to look at what we were really hungry for. Rather than telling us to lose weight with the *Nike* slogan "Just Do it!" she asked us to look at what our weight was really saying.

Ask yourself: "Will eating this food give me the nourishment (or love) I seek?" This is the real question.

Interactive wellness wheel

The first step in implementing a wellness program is to get in touch with your Primary Foods. Are you balanced? How is your health? Your finances? Your job? Your relationships?

The following "Interactive Wellness Wheel" offers you an opportunity to evaluate your overall state of consciousness.

INSTRUCTIONS:

Live life at the center, not on the circumference.
Paramahansa Yogananda

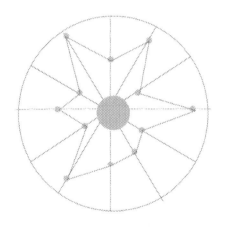

1. Place a dot on each spoke of the wheel on page 7 to indicate your level of balance in each category. Dots closer to the center indicate greater balance; dots closer to the circumference indicate less balance.

2. Connect the dots.

3. Take note of the areas that spike out toward the circumference (outer edge) of the circle. These are the areas that may need some time and attention. The

closer you are to the center,

the more balanced you are.

This assessment is to be completed without judgment. It is unlikely that you will end up with a small, perfect circle. More likely, you will end up with an asymmetrical star. If you feel you need help in balancing yourself, seek out a friend, or engage a counselor or health coach [1]

Before reading on, please stop and do this now.

Interactive Wellness Wheel

Live life at the center, not on the circumference

Chapter 2
BIO-INDIVIDUALITY

"One man's pain is another man's pleasure."
17th-century proverb

"Bio-Individuality," another term created by Joshua Rosenthal, founder of the *Institute for Integrative Nutrition*, refers to the unique and distinctive characteristics of your body/mind. Everybody has his or her own needs. My food plan may be very different from your food plan.

People are different. We have different ancestry, blood types, constitutions, lifestyles, metabolisms, body frames, genetic predispositions, cultural biases, and preferences. There is not one singular food plan that uniformly serves all of humanity. What may be good for me may not be good for you.

Because you have specific needs, according to your age, gender, size, and so on, it is important for you to listen to your body. Know what foods make you feel bad and what foods make you feel good.

Unfortunately, many processed foods, especially cakes, candies, chips, crackers, and cookies, have tricked you into thinking they make you feel good, even though the consequences of eating them are grave. They *taste* good. Food manufacturing companies spend millions of dollars on taste testers and scientists to create flavor additives that satisfy your *tongue*. (Read *The End of Overeating: Taking Control of the Insatiable American Appetite* by David A Kessler, MD., and *The Dorito Effect; the Surprising new truth about Food and Flavor* by Mark Schatzker.)

Some of these flavor additives are stimulating or addictive. Researchers have discovered pathways in the neurological network that are stimulated by certain tastes. Food manufacturers purposely add them to foods to get you hooked.

Some of these processed, sweetened, preserved foods are killing us. But they are doing so quietly. Sometimes it takes years for the consequences of our diets to manifest in physical symptoms. Only when the physiological degradation begins to manifest in diabetes, obesity, arthritis, fatigue, insomnia, thyroid problems, and heart conditions (to name a few), do we begin to take notice.

The good news is that you can reverse the effects of many of these age-related diseases. Just start where you are. It is never too late to change the habits that are contributing to your candy-coated, numbed out, bloated, pickled body.

Chapter 3

START HERE

To get in touch with the foods you truly desire and need, you first need to rid yourself of the processed foods that have taken over your senses.

Here are three ways to remove layers of false cravings and societal habits, and get in touch with who you really are and what you really need.

1) Enroll in a supervised "Cleanse" or "Detox" to rid your body of known toxins and replenish your body with fresh, whole foods. *(See Appendix for the author's "Seven-Day Kickstart Cleanse.")*

   You might also try an "Elimination Diet." To do this, you will want to remove a few specific foods most commonly found to be "allergenic." You remove these foods for three to four weeks. You then reintroduce each of these foods one at a time to see which ones may be causing reactive symptoms (like headaches, stomach pain, rashes, insomnia, depression, and lethargy, to name a few).

<u>Common allergenic foods:</u>
Gluten (wheat, oats, barley, rye,) dairy, eggs, soy, corn, coffee, alcohol, citrus fruits, nuts and seeds, and nightshade vegetables (tomatoes, peppers, eggplant, and white potatoes.)

2) Do "body scans" or "progressive relaxation" meditations to put you back in touch with your body. These are two meditation practices that can help you become more aware of your physical being. *(See Appendix, Meditation Techniques)*

3) Sweat. Move your body. This discharges toxins. The best exercise is the one you'll do. Anything. Something. Just move! Walk. Dance. Take a YOGA class. Join a softball league. Make it something you've always wanted to do or used to love to do. Make it a "want," not a "should."

Seek Professional Help

If you are really serious about taking control of your health, losing weight, or tackling whatever ails you, you will want to enlist the services of a functional, naturopathic, or integrative health professional. These physicians, nurses, health coaches, chiropractors, and nutritionists look at the causes behind your conditions, not just the symptoms.

Many health problems stem from digestive imbalance. Gastrointestinal issues have been linked to asthma and allergies, autoimmune disorders, skin conditions, arthritis, mood disorders, migraines, and kidney problems, to name a few.

Functional medicine uses a program called the "5 R's" to improve digestive imbalances. Sometimes, these techniques will completely resolve the problem. The elements of this program are:

1. Remove — the food stressors. Get rid of processed foods, gluten, sugars, dairy, and other allergenic foods that create symptoms. You may need to do an elimination diet for a couple of weeks to find out which foods are causing GI problems.
2. Replace missing digestive enzymes — add digestive enzyme supplements
3. Reinoculate — Help beneficial bacteria flourish by ingesting probiotic foods (sauerkraut, kimchee, kombucha, kefir) or Probiotic supplements.
4. Repair — the lining of the digestive tract. Add key nutrients that are often depleted, such as zinc, antioxidants (vitamins A, C & E), fish oil, and the amino acid, glutamine.
5. Rebalance — with plenty of sleep, exercise, and clean eating.

Once you have cleaned out your body, then you will be ready to start evaluating your true needs and create a food plan that suits your unique type and temperament.

"To thine own self be true."
From Hamlet by William Shakespeare

Chapter 4

WHAT DOES YOUR INTUITION SAY?

Once you have cleaned out your body, you can trust it. You are now in touch again with your essential nature. Your mind is clear.

Trusting yourself may not always be easy when best-seller books, "subject-matter" experts, talk show hosts, and headlines compete for attention with differing advice.

"It seems 50% of people approve of what I eat, and 50% don't," my friend Valarie said. "So I might as well just do what I want."

This gets back to bio-individuality, discussed in Chapter 2. The way you find your way out of conflicting dietary theories is to decide which food plan works best for *you*. What works best for you may be different from what worked for your friend, your father, or your future spouse.

Let me give you an example of how my intuition was recently challenged.

On a recent mini-vacation, we stayed in a resort in Klamath Falls, Oregon, where I attended a water aerobics class. Here, I met a woman whose job was to work with grocery chains on the ingredient labels for their in-house products. She was a strong and outgoing woman. We found a commonality in

"Nutrition" and were pretty much in sync until she said that she only eats frozen vegetables.

"Why?" I asked incredulously. I'm sure my face was plastered with judgment.

"They are fresh frozen," she said, "and are better for you than days old grocery greens."

"Maybe so," I replied, "but fresher can be bought at farmers' markets."

She disagreed.

I didn't push it any further, but later wish I had explained to her that the highest nutrient-density in a vegetable is realized from foods that are harvested as close to consumption as possible. So, the best vegetables you can eat are those you grow and harvest right before you eat them. Second best is locally grown, pesticide-free produce from your neighbors or neighborhood farmers' markets. Frozen vegetables endure several layers of time and processing from the original crop. I agree that, if not locally grown, the produce in supermarkets may not be fresh. But I did *not agree* that frozen is better.

Later, while studying "best food lists" for this book, I came across this recommendation from John's Hopkins Department of Medicine website in an article on "Post-Surgery Diet Tips"

Can I get the same nutritional value from frozen fruits and vegetables?

Yes. In fact, frozen foods are often more nutritious than fresh foods because they are usually picked ripe and quickly frozen.

http://pathology.jhu.edu/pc/TreatmentPostSurg Diet.php?area=tr

So, now what do I think? A random human and a reputable institution of higher learning have rattled my belief system.

I am in no better position than you to make a decision on this. In fact, sometimes "a little knowledge can be a dangerous thing." It can block your intuition and cause you to rely solely on your head to be the arbiter of all controversy.

Beyond intuition, the answer will come from your interpretation of the facts and your lifestyle. For example, do you have easily-accessible farmers' markets where you live? How big is your freezer? What *feels* right?

What is *your* answer to this conundrum?

I am sticking to my original premise because I live in California, the agricultural center of the world. Here, produce is fresh and plentiful almost all year round. In the summer, I grow my own crops. I've turned my back yard into an informal neighborhood farm. For five months a year, as many as eight families work the land behind my house and harvest fresh crops for our families. It's our own post-war Victory Garden.

Tangent

How is the choice you need to make in this situation any different from all other decisions you make in life?

What you choose to eat will reflect your upbringing, your personal circumstances, your knowledge, your environment, and even your politics.

You would do well to recognize this when you criticize other peoples' choices and preferences. Who are *you* to judge?

Chapter 5

CRITERIA FOR EVALUATING DIETARY THEORIES

New dietary studies hit the headlines every week. I kept delaying the completion of this book because of the constant flow of "late breaking dietary news." I wanted to make sure I was bringing you timely and current information.

In fact, the week I finally decided to stop writing, the World Health Organization (WHO) came out with findings drafted by 22 international experts that linked red meat, bacon, sausage, and other processed meats with cancer. The *Time* magazine that followed, featured two strips of bacon on its cover with an expose called "The War on Delicious." (by Jeffery Kluger, November 9, 2015.) Not surprisingly, the $95 billion US beef industry and many others are questioning these conclusions and are mounting a campaign to refute the data.

So we must stay continuously informed. Know that there are usually two sides to every story. The three constants I've found in an ever-changing nutritional world are *moderation, variety, and vegetables.*

Other questions to ask when assessing a dietary theory are:

1. What theories do longitudinal studies support?
2. Who financed the study that supported the theory?

3. Have there been any "meta-analyses" to support the theory?

Longitudinal Studies

Longitudinal studies are those that have been going on for a long time.

One of my favorites is *The Framingham Study*. It was begun in 1948 with 5,209 adults in Framingham, Massachusetts. It is now in its third generation of participants.

In the 1950s, it was believed that clogging of the arteries was just a normal part of aging, and there was nothing you could do about it. This study that showed that diet, exercise, and aspirin reduce heart risk. In fact, this is the study that originated the term "Risk Factor."

Another important longitudinal study is *The Nurses' Health Study*. Initiated by the National Institutes of Health, it now enjoys the collaboration of Harvard and other prestigious institutions.

"Started in 1976 and expanded in 1989, the information provided by the 238,000 dedicated nurse-participants has led to many new insights on health and disease. While the prevention of cancer is still a primary focus, the study has also produced landmark data on cardiovascular disease, diabetes, and many other conditions. Most importantly, these **studies have shown that diet, physical activity, and other**

lifestyle factors can powerfully promote better health." *(Bold added by author for emphasis.)*

From The Nurses' Study Website:
www.channing.harvard.edu/nh

Who profits from nutritional information?

It is important to know who finances the studies that prove divergent nutritional theories. We must know if they make a profit from the information they are disseminating.

It is easy to dismiss a web or postcard promo that says something like:

> *"With this supplement, you will lose 12 pounds in one week. Just three installments of $14.95. Money Back Guarantee."*

It is *not* easy to find out who finances the studies that make headlines. You have to be very motivated to track down which company contributes to the foundation that funds the research establishment that executes the study that "proves" the validity of one nutritional theory over another.

An example of this was revealed by Marion Nestle, Professor of Nutrition, Food Studies and Public Health at New York University. She found that "roughly 85% of independently funded studies find strong correlations between soda drinking and poor health. Roughly 85% of the studies that are funded by the soda industry, find soda to be harmless."

Meta-analyses

"Meta-analyses" look at multiple studies with many participants, to try to substantiate a hypothesis. These, of course, can go both ways. Studies are always proving and disproving each other.

The meta-analysis correlating consumption of meats with cancer, was conducted by a respected World Health Organization subsidiary, the International Agency for Research on Cancer (IARC), that evaluated 800 published papers.

One meta-analysis I like, which appeared in the *American Journal of Clinical Nutrition* in January 2010, looked at almost 350,000 subjects in 21 studies to assess the correlation between saturated fat consumption and cardiovascular disease. The conclusion was that intake of saturated fat was *not* associated with an increased risk of heart disease or stroke.

This belief is echoed by the American Heart Association, which has revised its guidelines and moved away from formerly strict recommendations to lower fat intake.

Chapter 6

GOOD FATS, BAD FATS

We start our nutritional discussion with a look at dietary fats.

I grew up in a generation where fat was the bad guy.

Nathan Pritikin, a famous nutritionist of the 1970s/early 80s, believed that fat was responsible for cancer, stroke, and heart disease. My own father attended his "Pritikin Longevity Center," and my mother dutifully created menus with no more than 10% fat. (Today, the fat allowance in your diet is up to 30%.) Whole eggs were discarded in favor of egg whites, and "low-fat" products dominated our kitchen. Little did we know that the margarine and low-fat mayonnaise were filled with lethal trans fats, and the low-fat crackers and boxed foods contained added sugar to compensate for the taste loss from the removal of fats.

The FDA banned artificial trans fats, which come from partially hydrogenated oils, in June 2015 after an eleven-year battle. Trans fat is a liver-damaging, artery-clogging, weight-adding artificial substance that began with Crisco in the 50s and continues to be used in coffee creamers, cake frostings, packaged chips, fried foods, and microwave popcorn.

At this writing, foods that contain trans fats include Girl Scout cookies, Quaker Oats Chewy Granola Bars, saltine crackers, Fig Newtons, Ritz crackers, fortune cookies, and Special K's entire line of health/weight loss food [2]

This is *not* the fat I'm suggesting you eat.

Most nutritional scientists agree that trans fats are bad. It is estimated that their removal from the market is preventing 20,000 heart attacks and 7,000 deaths from heart disease each year.

Most nutritional scientists agree that monounsaturated fats are good. Monounsaturated fats include avocados, salmon, almonds, walnuts, flax seed, and olive and canola oils. These fats have been linked to a lower risk of heart disease and decreased inflammation. (Canola oils are often contaminated so you should purchase organic versions of this oil).

Nutritional scientists *do not* agree on the value of saturated fats. Saturated fats are more controversial. Saturated fats include dairy products, animal protein, coconut, and palm oils.

Those with vulnerable or missing gall bladders should definitely go easy on the intake of all fats.

If you talk to a vegetarian, you will be told that fatty animal proteins, including dairy, will raise cholesterol and increase the risk of heart disease and cancer. (Read *The China Study: The Most Comprehensive Study of Nutrition Ever Conducted and the Startling Implications for Diet, Weight Loss, and Long-Term Health* by Thomas and T. Colin Campbell.)

If you talk to a traditional foods or Paleo advocate, you will be told that traditional fats are anti-microbial, anti-viral, and anti-cancer, and they raise bone mineral density and HDL (the good component of cholesterol). (Read *Deep Nutrition: Why Your Genes Need Traditional Food* by Catherine and Luke Shanahan.)

See Appendix for an elaboration of these key dietary theories.

Chapter 7

SUGAR BLUES

"Like heroin, cocaine, and caffeine, sugar is an addictive, destructive drug, yet we consume it daily."

William Dufty, author of *Sugar Blues*

Sugar, not fat, is the biggest toxin in our current diet. Sugar is not unlike poison in its effect on our body. It is a harmful and addictive substance.

Excessive consumption of sugar has been shown to cause hypoglycemia, premature aging, tooth decay, arthritis, asthma, cancer (of the ovaries, rectum, prostrate, kidneys and liver), heart disease, multiple sclerosis, hemorrhoids, appendicitis, gallstones, and irritable bowel syndrome, to name a few. Sugar increases anxiety and depression and decreases immune function, tissue elasticity and function, absorption of calcium and magnesium, learning capacity, and adrenal function.

Nancy Appleton, author of *Lick the Sugar Habit*, has produced a list called *146 Reasons Why Sugar is Ruining Your Health (www. nancyappleton.com.)* Print it out. The number of ways sugar adversely affects your functioning will astound you.

The average American consumes more than 100 pounds of sugar in a year compared to just about eight pounds of broccoli.

Most Americans eat about 30 teaspoons of sugar per day. That's three to four times the recommended amount.

Big Soda

One of the most insidious purveyors of sugar is soda. The average 12 oz. can contains about 9 teaspoons of sugar.

About 20 minutes after you drink a can of soda pop, your blood sugar spikes, causing an insulin reaction that directs your liver to convert the sugar into fat.

After about 40 minutes, your pupils become dilated, your blood pressure rises, and your liver starts to deposit more sugar into your blood stream.

Over time, daily sodas will start to compromise most of your body. Your risk of type 2 diabetes and obesity will increase. Your memory will decrease. You will have a greater chance of developing heart disease. Your lungs will become vulnerable to chronic obstructive pulmonary disorder (COPD), and your teeth will rot.

For more on this, read *Soda Politics; Taking on Big Soda (and Winning)* by Marion Nestle (2015)

Soda addiction is a difficult habit to break. If you suffer from this addiction, try infused waters. Or better yet, just plain water. Start by just tapering off. Make rules for yourself that you can live with, like: " No drinking Sodas at Meals." Whenever you are trying to reduce your consumption of a pleasurable food source, it is best not to think of eliminating it totally forever. You can always have one now and then as a treat.

Can I be happy without sugar?

If, when you eat sugar, you crave more, you eat more, and you can't control your consumption, then you are probably addicted to it.

I am a sugar addict. Sometimes, I feel there is no pleasure greater than that offered by the taste of something sweet. Even with my knowledge of sugar's toxicity, I often fall off the wagon. Fortunately, this occurs much less frequently than in the past.

Our body is hard-wired to prefer sugar. Neil deGrasse Tyson, renowned astrophysicist, thinks one of the most astounding facts is that the atoms that make up the human body are traceable to the stars. Sugar molecules have been found in stars! If we are basically derived from stardust, and sugar is a key component of stardust, it is no small surprise that we are drawn to this substance. It is essentially in our DNA.

Food companies have identified our pre-disposition for sugar and magnified it, surreptitiously stashing sugar in most processed foods and secretly addicting us.

After I eat sugar, I feel miserable, sleep poorly, get depressed, have less energy, and judge myself harshly for my transgression.

I am at my happiest when I am off sugar. It usually takes a whole week to clean out sugar from my system after a lapse. (Most people require 21 days to detoxify from sugar.) When I am clean, I have more energy, I think more clearly, I sleep more soundly, and I have more endurance.

Breaking this addiction is not easy. Some research shows that sugar can be as addictive as cocaine. Sugar addiction has both physiological and psychological components. It could be the result of mineral, vitamin, or hormonal imbalances, or yeast overgrowth, or digestive distress. Or you may be eating sugar to numb pain, manage stress, or to meet other emotional needs.

It is unlikely that you can cure your sugar addiction with will power. Attempts to control your cravings, emotions, diet, and relationships with will power only lead to despair. Control is *not* the solution to sugar addiction.

Because I am a sugar addict, I must go cold turkey and cannot even have a taste of it while I am detoxifying. It is like an alcoholic who cannot tempt fate with even one drink.

There are many programs that can assist you in kicking the habit. The best combine emotional support, self-observation, crowding out cravings with a diet of whole foods, and acceptance.

Some of my favorite books on the subject are:

- *Lick the Sugar Habit,* by Nancy Appleton
- *Potatoes not Prozac,* by Kathleen Des Maisons
- *Sugar Blues,* by William Dufty
- *Sugar Shock,* by Connie Bennett
- *Overcoming Sugar Addiction,* by Karly Randoph Pitman
- *The Mood Cure,* by Julia Ross
- *Simply Sugar Free,* by Sue Brown

Also, feel free to contact me at <u>theodora@wilnerweb.com</u> for support based on my true-life experience. On request, I can send you handouts produced by the *Institute for Integrative Nutrition*® called "Ten Tips for Dealing with Sugar Addiction" and "How Much Sugar Are You Consuming?"

Chapter 8

EAT WHOLE FOODS

I am about to share a secret with you. It is a secret you already know.

I offer you a one-sentence dietary guideline that will change your life as it has changed mine.

It will help you lose weight, reverse type II diabetes, improve thyroid function, reduce your risk of heart disease, decrease depression and anxiety, minimize arthritis pain, reduce back pain, and help you feel better, look better, and live longer.

Here it is:

> *"Eat whole, organic,*
> *locally and responsibly grown foods*
> *savored slowly."*

That's it.

If you eat this way, you do not need to worry about dietary theories or calories or ingredient lists. You don't need to worry about conflicting headlines, subject matter experts, and talk show hosts and guests whose information may or may not be based on a solid body of evidence. You simply eat fresh.

This way of eating is supported by some of the nation's most renowned food and lifestyle experts: Daniel Amen, Andrea

Beaman, Mark Bittman, Colin Campbell, Sally Fallon, Joel Fuhrman, Mark Hyman, David Kessler, Marion Nestle, Nina Planck, Michael Pollan, John Robbins, Joshua Rosenthal, Catherine Shanahan, Andrew Weil, Walter Willett, and David Wolfe to name a few.

Eating whole contributes to your *feeling* whole. Feeling whole is feeling complete, lacking for nothing, having everything you need within you. When you are complete, you are balanced. You enjoy life fully and view everything from the perspective of love, joy, light and delight.

When *I* am balanced, I feel better about life. Everything I do and say comes from a place of higher awareness. I am happier, healthier, and more effective.

Let's dissect this one sentence dietary guideline to see how it translates to practice.

What is a whole food?

Whole foods are perishable. Whole foods rot. Whole foods come from the earth, not from a box. A whole food is not a whole pizza.

Dr. Goli Sahba, MD, a functional doctor in Sacramento who was instrumental in shaping my food habits, told me to eat leafy greens at every meal. It is the best health advice I have ever received.

Leafy greens carry the greatest amount and variety of nutrients and are high in fiber. Consuming large quantities of leafy greens (e.g., BIG salads) will help you crowd out less filling and nutritious alternatives.

If eating leafy greens seems challenging to do at breakfast, all you need to do is add a large handful of "power greens" to your smoothies or omelets. "Power greens" and other already-packaged and cleaned leafy greens are a new wonder food, which I first discovered at *Trader Joes*. They have now made their way into the produce department of most major food chains. You can now buy triple-washed collard greens, spinach, kale, and chard in packaged containers everywhere.

I think these bagged, cleaned greens are God's nutritional gift to working parents, anyone with time constraints, and non-cooks who don't like buying and preparing food. Now you can eat healthfully without the arduous prep time required for washing, drying, and cutting fresh veggies. Just rip open a bag and pour onto a plate, or into a soup pot, or steam in one inch of boiling water for a few minutes.

These packaged greens are certainly not as fresh as those at the farmers' markets. But if I had to choose packaged fresh vegetables over having a meal without vegetables, or a meal with frozen or canned vegetables, I would choose the packaged greens.

What is organic/pesticide-free?

"Pesticides are… of concern to us all. If we are going to live so intimately with these chemicals, eating and drinking them, taking them into the very marrow of our bones -

we had better know something about their nature and their power."
Rachel Carson, From Silent Spring, 1962
(The book that launched the American environmental movement)

Organic and pesticide-free foods are free of synthetic fertilizers and the bug sprays that are destroying bee colonies, causing cancer, and polluting our earth, air, and water.

For a food to be certified as "organic," it must comply with national standards. These standards require, among other things, that the grower not use pesticides for three years prior to certification. A "pesticide-free" farmer is either in the process of becoming organic or cannot afford the fees or manage the paperwork and time associated with "organic" certification.

I have a very good friend who once told me that she did not believe in buying organic or pesticide-free food.

"Too expensive?" I asked, knowing that this is a true and legitimate deterrent.

"No," she said, "I just don't like eating bugs."

"You can always wash off or boil away any 'unwelcome protein,'" I countered.

She grimaced and scrunched up her face. "But I'd *know* the bugs had been there."

"So you'd rather eat pesticides?" I asked.

"Sure," she said, "I just wash them off."

"Sometimes washing does not remove the pesticide residue that has been absorbed into the fruit," I countered.

"Well," she concluded, "most of us eat these fruits and vegetables all the time, and we're all doing just fine."

I was aghast at this mentality but realize her viewpoint is that of the majority. The corporate farms that bring us most of our produce do not advertise the poisonous coatings on their crops.

Factory Farm Waste

Factory farms create uniformly sized, bug-free, plastic wrapped, pretty crops that appeal to the consumer even though they may be at the expense of sustainability and long-term health.

Thousands of pounds of crops are tossed a year if they do not conform to consumers' "prettiness" standard. Some estimate that more than a third of the food grown around the world is uneaten. There is nothing wrong with these "naturally imperfect" fruits.

With so much hunger in the world, it is hard to believe that this much food is going to waste.

The "Ugly Food Movement" is now sending these misshapen crops to certain supermarket chains to sell at reduced prices. France, Canada, Great Britain, and Australia have led the charge, but the U.S. is beginning to follow this trend. I am proud to say that my locally-owned Sacramento food chain, *Raley's,* is participating in this experiment.

According to the United States Environmental Protection Agency (EPA,) there *are* detrimental effects to the nervous and endocrine systems from certain pesticides. Others are known to be carcinogenic (cancer-causing.) The EPA assesses risks associated with individual pesticides based on arbitrary levels of consumption. These levels are far less than the number of vegetables and fruits eaten by vegetarians and other mindful consumers.

For those of you who share my friend's distaste for bugs, please be aware of "The Dirty Dozen." These specific crops have been found to contain the highest concentration of pesticide residues. It is unlikely that you will be able to remove the pesticide residue from these particular crops through scrubbing. How do you "scrub" a strawberry? A cherry tomato?

If you do not want to buy organic or pesticide-free versions of these listed fruits and vegetables, then just avoid them.

"The Clean Fifteen," on the other hand, have been shown to be free of pesticide residue, so these can be purchased without the "organic" or "pesticide-free" nomenclature. Both lists are provided below.

The "Dirty Dozen" (+3)

Avoid these fruits and vegetables or buy organic or pesticide-free
Apples
Celery
Cherry tomatoes
Cucumbers

Grapes

Nectarines

Peaches

Potatoes

Snap peas

Spinach

Strawberries

Sweet bell peppers

> \+ Three additional surprising culprits:
>
> Collard greens
>
> Hot peppers
>
> Kale

The "Clean Fifteen"

Buying conventional produce is fine. The following items do not need to be organic.

Asparagus

Avocados

Cabbage

Cantaloupe

Cauliflower

Eggplant

Grapefruit

Kiwi

Mangoes

Onion

Papayas

Pineapples

Sweet corn

Sweet peas

Sweet potatoes

These lists come from *The Environmental Working Group (www.ewg.org)*.a non- profit, non-partisan organization dedicated to protecting human health and the environment. For a small donation, wallet cards are available with these listings.

If you don't have these wallet cards or lists with you when you go shopping, you might avoid any fruit or vegetable without a thick skin or that grows close to or on the ground. These crops are sprayed more heavily or are more "absorbent" and are more susceptible to retention of pesticides.

Why locally grown?

Crops and animals that are purchased from your neighborhood farmer or farmers' market are the freshest. The fresher the food is, the higher the nutrient value.

Also, they have not been shipped or flown or trucked from far off lands or across the nation. Transporting crops from far away increases our dependence on fossil fuels which compromises air quality as well as freshness.

Supporting local growers also supports your local economy. This is consistent with the idea of "thinking globally and acting locally." With this philosophy, you consider the wellness of the entire planet while promoting the wellness, solidarity, and support of your local community.

What is responsibly-grown?

Whole Foods' founder, John Mackey, who did not believe the term "Organic" went far enough, coined this term. Organic does not address issues like soil health, farm worker and animal welfare, waste reduction, and energy efficiency.

My one-sentence dietary guideline to eat healthy whole foods will be undermined by farms and ranches that do not support the growth of diversified, nutrient-dense, healthy foods. If the food chain is skewed to favor profit over people, the people will lose.

One example of this is corn "monoculture." Corn grown for grain accounts for almost one-quarter of the harvested crop acres in this county. Corn is used primarily for ethanol, animal feed, and high-fructose corn syrup.

Corn "monoculture" is not the best way to use our land. It is not being used to feed people, which most people assume is the main objective of agriculture.

Corn is also a land, water, and fertilizer hog. This massive corn industry (97 million acres—an area roughly the size of California) depletes natural resources while delivering relatively little food and nutrition to people.

Jonathan Foley, Ph.D., Executive Director of the California Academy of Sciences, gives us a picture of what a "re-imagined" diverse agricultural system would look like. He asks us to grow corn together with many kinds of grains, fruits, vegetables, grazing and prairie lands:

"Production practices <should> blend the best of conventional, conservation, biotech, and organic farming. Subsidies would be aimed at rewarding farmers for producing more healthy, nutritious food while preserving rich soil, clean water, and thriving landscapes for future generations. This system would feed more people, employ more farmers, and be more sustainable and more resilient than anything we have today."

It is important to point out that criticisms of the current corn system are *not* intended to malign hard-working farmers on whom we depend for our sustenance.

Consider these additional facts:

- More than 5 billion pounds of pesticides are used worldwide each year. Pesticides are not healthy for humans and other living things.
- Bees and butterflies are crucial for pollinating over 65% of the world's crops. Their populations are in serious decline from pesticide exposure.
- Agriculture uses 70% of the world's fresh water.
- Farming is responsible for up to 12% of the world's human-generated greenhouse gas emissions.

Following is a description of responsibly grown qualities in farming, mostly adapted from the *Whole Foods* website. It should be noted that, not surprisingly, these characteristics are in dispute and are under strenuous attack from agribusiness.

Healthy Soil —The healthier the soil, the healthier the crop. Examples of practices that improve the soil include composting, crop rotation, and cover crops.

Water Conservation —We in California have been plagued by drought. It is not a pretty sight. Trees are dying, lawns are brown, lands that cannot sustain crops are fallow, and all of us have restrictions on water usage. Forest fires abound; in the summer of 2015, two fires came within one half mile of my home. Responsible farming practices must protect and conserve water. Examples include rainwater collection and drip irrigation.

Ecosystems and Biodiversity — Responsible farming practices protect native species and protect beneficial insects from harmful chemicals.

Air and Energy — Responsible farms reduce air pollution and conserve energy. This may include use of renewable energy sources such as wind and solar power.

Pest Management — Responsible farms reduce pesticide use with its risks to consumers, farm workers, wildlife and the environment and use methods such as "integrative pest management" to protect crops from insect invasions.

Farm worker Welfare — What would we eat without the backbreaking work of the laborers who harvest our crops? We must protect them. Responsibly grown farms promote safe working conditions and fair compensation.

Animal Welfare — Ranchers who follow ethical standards, feed their animals a varied diet in open pastures their whole lives (100% grass fed). Because their environment is more natural, farmers do not need to pump their animals with the antibiotics that protect them from the contamination in overcrowded stalls, and have produced an antibiotic-resistant crisis in the health care delivery system. Nor do they pump them with growth hormones to speedily increase their size and profitability.

The Horror of Factory Farmed Meats

Watch this 10-minute PETA Film: *Meet your Meat.* In this horrifying narration, Alec Baldwin exposes the truth behind humanity's cruelest invention — the factory farm. See how the factory farms that bring you beef, pork, chicken, and turkeys treat their animals.

Most of these animals live in miserable, overcrowded conditions. To reduce the consequences of the hostility of animals bred by these conditions, pigs' tails and chickens' beaks are amputated without anesthesia.

One reason chickens are fed antibiotics is to protect them against the bacteria from those that drop dead from living in these overcrowded, horrific conditions. Chicken barns are only required to be cleaned once a month. That's when you find the dead chickens on the floor.

When a cow demonstrates infirmity, they run a hose of water up its nose to revive it for slaughter. Slaughter is uniformly brutal and slow. The animals suffer.

Humanely-raised animals are raised in fenced-in fields, not crowded barns. It is important that the "100%" marker precedes the words "grass-fed." In factory farms, cows are brought inside in the last few weeks of their lives, confined in small spaces, and fattened up on a corn-dominated diet. [3]

What does "savoring" have to do with all this?

We are a rushed society. We need to learn how to slow down and savor all things – food, children, and time. We need to take time out to smell the roses. Literally. The "slow food movement" invites you to do things as well as possible rather than as fast as possible.

Slow eating is also better for your digestion.

The digestive process begins in the mouth. Saliva helps digest your food. The more you chew your food, the better able you are to digest what you eat. When you gulp your food, you are more likely to experience gastrointestinal distress such as indigestion and flatulence. Sometimes, when you swallow large pieces of un-chewed food, your immune system mistakes it for an invader and attacks it.

And of course, when you take your time to chew, you are better able to enjoy the tastes and smells of the food.

Try these techniques to slow down your eating.

> Before eating: Wash your hands. Stretch and breathe. Say a blessing. (See Food Blessing by Thich Nhat Hanh)

<u>During the meal:</u> Eat one bite at a time. Put your fork down between bites. To get started in this practice, try chewing each bite 25 times.

<u>After the meal:</u> Sit for an extra moment. Breathe. Offer gratitude.

Food Blessing

by Thich Nhat Hanh
Modified by the author

This food is the gift of the whole universe,
the earth, the sky, and much hard work.

May we live in a way that makes
us worthy to receive it.

May we eat only foods that
nourish and prevent illness.

May we eat in moderation.

Thank you for this food.

May it further our commitment
to sustainability and grace.

Chapter 9

BEST FOODS

This section features a compilation of food recommendations from different sources. There are numerous dietary theories, and each recommends a slightly different set of foods. Some dietary recommendations even contradict each other. For most, there is some overlap. For instance, vegetables are the singular group for which there is no controversy. All dietary pundits believe that vegetables should be the corner stone of a healthy food plan.

If you are reading this book a few years after the publication date, these lists may have changed. Nutritional science is a rapidly changing field.

You want to pay attention to the list that responds to your bio-individuality and remediates any conditions you have.

Best Food Guides

The ANDI Guide

ANDI stands for "Aggregate Nutrient Density Index." Joel Fuhrman, MD, who created the "Fruitarian" food plan, created this scale. The ANDI Chart rates foods on a scale from 1-1000 based on nutrient content. These scores are calculated by looking at vitamins, minerals, phytochemicals (plant nutrients), and antioxidants (molecules that inhibit cell damage from oxidation).

The ANDI Guide rates almost 100 foods.

> <u>The ten best scoring foods, highest to lower:</u>
> Kale and collards set the bar with the highest score of 1,000. Next we have bok choy, spinach, Brussels sprouts, arugula, cabbage, romaine lettuce, broccoli, and cauliflower.

> <u>The ten worst scoring foods, from lowest to slightly higher:</u>
> Cola, French fries, olive oil, vanilla ice cream, American cheese, potato chips, Swiss cheese, apple juice, white bread and white pasta.

> *Author's comments: Dr. Fuhrman places olive oil on the bottom of the list because he believes good fat can be better derived through nuts, avocados, salmon, and omega 3's.*

> *As stated in Chapter 6, most dietary experts believe olive oil should also be included in this category of healthy fats. These monounsaturated fats are important for insulation, building brain cells, assisting in vitamin absorption, regulating the production of hormones, improving the health of skin, hair, and nails, and reducing heart disease.*

YOGA Eating Guide

- **Sattvic** foods are to be consumed in abundance. They keep the mind clear and the body well. Sattvic foods do no harm. Examples of Sattvic foods are water, legumes, vegetables, fruits, nuts, raw milk, ghee, fresh cottage cheese (paneer), yogurt, and honey.

- **Rajasic** foods are stimulating. Sometimes they are good (as before a marathon) and sometimes they are not good (as before sleep). Rajasic foods include chocolate, spicy and salty foods, and caffeinated drinks.

- **Tamasic** foods slow you down. They are detrimental to the body and mind. They can lead to aggressiveness and irritability and are often obtained in a way that harms another organism. These foods should be avoided except in times of pain or to alleviate suffering. Examples of Tamasic foods are animals, onions, garlic, mushrooms, alcoholic beverages, blue cheese, and opium.

Taste Guidelines

In Japanese culture, it is *taste* that determines the make up of a meal. It is the unification of five tastes in every meal — saltiness, sourness, sweetness, bitterness, and Unami ("savory") — that distinguishes a Japanese meal.

Japanese chefs also value the importance of "Shun" in their menus. "Shun" is similar to the concept of eating locally grown, but it is more precise. With "Shun," you eat foods in the exact season in the exact moment of the year when they are the freshest and taste their best.

Best Food Lists

Following are a few of the "best foods to eat" lists. I only chose food plans offered by reputable practitioners, academics, or non-profit organizations. I deliberately stayed away from "celebrity" diets. My commentary on each follows in italics.

10 Great Health Foods by *the Mayo Clinic* (in alphabetical order)

- Almonds
- Apples
- Blueberries
- Broccoli
- Beans
- Salmon
- Spinach
- Sweet potatoes
- Vegetable juice

10 Best Foods by *Nutrition Action*

- Sweet potatoes
- Mangoes
- Unsweetened Greek yogurt
- Broccoli
- Wild salmon
- Whole grain "crisp breads"

- Garbanzo beans
- Watermelon
- Butternut squash
- Leafy greens

Author's comments: I disagree with the relegation of leafy greens to the bottom of this list. My protestations are muted by the fact that I admire the organization that sponsors this list. The Center for Science in the Public Interest (CSPI) is our best consumer nutrition advocacy organization. It accepts no advertising, corporate funds, or government grants.

10 Best Foods for Your Heart by *Health.com.*

- Oatmeal
- Salmon
- Avocado
- Olive oil
- Nuts
- Berries
- Legumes
- Spinach
- Flax seed
- Soybeans

Author's comments: Some would quarrel with the inclusion of soy on this list. Vegetarians love soy because it has one of the highest levels of plant protein. But soy is one of the foods (along with corn, eggs, milk, nuts, shellfish and wheat) that are most likely to cause allergic reactions.

One study shows that soy influences the growth of estrogen-dependent breast cancer tumors (Oxford University Press, 2004). If you insist on eating soy, stick to the whole beans (aka "edamame") and the fermented variations (aka "tempeh")

Anti-Inflammatory Foods by *The Arthritis Foundation*

- Leafy green vegetables: Swiss chard, bok choy
- Fish: salmon, tuna, sardine, anchovies, and other cold water fish
- Fruits: deep colored berries and greens, especially blueberries, blackberries, cherries, strawberries, spinach, kale, and broccoli
- Nuts: walnuts, pine nuts, pistachios, and almonds
- Beans
- Extra virgin olive oil
- Onions

Avoid:

- Nightshades – eggplant, tomatoes, peppers, and tomatoes. However, scientific evidence on this is inconclusive. Try cutting these foods from your diet for two weeks and see if symptoms improve.
- Processed foods
- Salt
- Sugar

Author's comments: I have had osteoarthritis for about 10 years. I inherited it from my father. As long as I can remember, his top knuckles were perpendicular to the rest of his fingers. I am no longer able to open jars, I often feel stiff when I get out of bed in the morning, and I ache if I eat too much sugar. Sometimes, rainy weather makes me feel creaky. But I do not feel pain. I do not feel worse when I eat nightshade vegetables, which are the mainstay of my summer garden. I credit my YOGA practice with keeping me flexible and pain free.

Best Meal Plans for **Diabetes** by the *American Diabetes Association*

- Vegetables
- Whole grains
- Fruits
- Non-fat, low sugar dairy products
- Beans
- Lean meats
- Poultry
- Fish

Johns Hopkins' Dietary Guidelines for **Cancer**

- Fruits and vegetables
- Fresh fish
- Whole grains
- Limit saturated fats (lamb, beef, organ meats, cheese, cream)

- Avoid alcohol, caffeine, and sugar

American Cancer Society Guidelines for Nutrition

- Choose foods and drinks in amounts that help you get to and maintain a healthy weight
- Limit how much processed and red meat you eat
- Eat at least 2 ½ cups of vegetables and fruits each day
- Choose whole grains instead of refined grain products
- Drink no more than one alcoholic drink/day for women and two drinks/day for men

Best Foods for **Digestive Distress**

The "FODMAP" Diet

FODMAPs are "short chain" carbohydrates (fermentable oligo-di-monosaccharides and polyols) that may not be digested or absorbed well by the small intestine. SIBO (small intestine bacterial overgrowth) can cause diarrhea, constipation, gas, bloating, and irritable bowel syndrome.

The FODMAPS plan is confusing because one must eliminate many healthy foods such as apples, peaches, cauliflower, sugar snap peas, hummus, garlic, and more. The good news is that this is intended as a short-term diet; normal eating may be resumed when symptoms disappear.

Stanford produces a great FODMAP handout. It includes both an explanation and a list of foods to avoid. (To print out this list, Google: "FODMAPS, Stanford" in your browser.)

Best Foods for **Weight Loss** *by the author*

- First thing in your stomach in morning:
- Water, lemon and hot water, or 1 teaspoon of apple cider vinegar in water to clean yourself out and aid digestion.
- All vegetables, with an emphasis on leafy greens
- All fruits with an emphasis on organic berries, apples with cinnamon, and citrus (if not allergic)
- Wild salmon, sardines, and sugar-free gefilte fish
- Humanely-raised animal protein
- Eggs
- Broth-based soups
- Salsa and hummus
- Herbal and green tea
- 1 tablespoon of sauerkraut or kimchee (probiotic) with meals
- Filtered water: as much and as often as you can drink until 6pm

Chapter 10

CRAVINGS

Best food lists, like best intentions, are often sabotaged by cravings.

I have been plagued by cravings my whole life. Cravings have led me to binge, to eat when I'm not hungry, to make inappropriate food choices, and to feel awful about myself. I refer to my cravings as "demonic" because they take over my senses and strip me of all reason.

What causes these cravings and what can we do about them?

According to Rena Greenberg, author of *The Craving Cure* (McGraw Hill, 2007), there are five reasons for food cravings:

1. Low blood sugar or physical hunger
   Caused by not eating regularly or eating the wrong foods

2. Malnutrition
   Caused by not getting enough nutrients

3. Food sensitivities
   Caused by preferences for certain foods (usually refined carbohydrates), which both trigger and relieve the craving

4. Unresolved emotional issues

Caused by unresolved sadness, anger, boredom, or loneliness

5. Stress

Caused by an inability to be resilient and accepting.

Later in the book (see "Seek the Dark," Chapter 15), we will look at the importance of digging deep into our psyches to expose the wounds that often lead to cravings. Cravings may not be released until we can identify the triggers and repair these deep-seated wounds.

There *are* some things we can do right now to control some cravings.

1) **Drink water.** Dehydration can trigger a false sense of hunger. If you get a craving, head to your clean water source. Drink. Drink a full glass of water. Drink often. It has been said that when your mouth is dry and you feel thirsty, you are already dehydrated.

2) **Keep busy with people you like.** Friends are our chosen families. Do not allow boredom and loneliness to take hold. If you seek the comfort of friends, it will reduce your desire to seek comfort in pudding and potato chips.

3) **Decrease stress by moving your body.** Exercise is the surest stress reliever. The best exercise is the one you'll do. Dance. Walk. Jump rope. Just make sure you

choose an activity you like and want to do. (See more on this in "Walking and More," Chapter 22.)

4) **Balance the foods you eat**. Too much sugar may cause cravings for meat; too many salads may cause cravings for too many warm foods.

5) **Avoid bewitching aromas** when you are tired or sad. Avoid bakeries and routes that take you by those tantalizing smells or "must have" food stops. It is probably not a good idea to go grocery shopping after a frustrating day at work.

6) **Honor your ancestors** without dying. Foods from our past are often tempting. If you are missing Grandma's chocolate chip cookies or Mom's tapioca pudding, perhaps there's a way you can create healthier versions of these recipes.

7) **Pay attention to hormonal fluctuations.** PMS, pregnancy, and menopause often produce a unique set of cravings, especially for sweets. Have fruits available during these times.

Water, Fat and Weight

- The kidneys depend on water for their functioning. When the kidneys do not get enough water, they punt some of their responsibility over to the liver. This sidetracks the liver from its main function of metabolizing fat.
- Drinking enough water helps stop fluid retention. Without enough water, the body feels threatened and starts holding onto water outside the cells. This can manifest as swollen hands and feet.
- Overweight people need more water than thinner people. They have larger metabolic loads.
- Water helps flush out waste matter.
- Drinking enough water prevents constipation. When the body does not have enough water, it may divert water from the colon. This can result in constipation.

Chapter 11

THE FOOD PYRAMID IS WRONG

I have heard, but cannot confirm, that the original food pyramid was a chart that originated in barns to guide farmers in the proper care and feeding of pigs.

Government Guidelines for Nutrition come from the United States Department of Agriculture (USDA). They published their first Food Guide Pyramid in 1992. In 2005, the pyramid was reconfigured into vertical segments and exercise was added, but there were few changes in the food recommendations. In 2011, the food pyramid morphed into a round plate. This most recent iteration made two important changes: 1) It acknowledged the importance of vegetables by increasing the recommended amount, and 2) It replaced the words "Meat, Poultry, Fish" with the more generic designation of "Protein." Unfortunately, it still recommends Dairy as a separate recommended food source. This beverage designation, off to the side, should more appropriately be replaced with "Water."

Through all its permutations, this government graphic retains the same basic recommendation for eating the majority of calories in grains. Many nutritionists believe that these food pyramids, with their emphasis on grain consumption, are among the causes of the current obesity epidemic.

Grains are fattening. Also, the consumer does not fully get the meaning of "whole grain." Food manufacturers pushing "natural" non-whole grain breads, and "healthy" sugar-enriched cereals fuel this misunderstanding. These meaningless marketing descriptors have given the consumer permission to binge on empty calories.

Large corporate farms have had the strongest influence over the USDA's dietary guidelines. Why would the consumption of grains — even if whole — form the bottom tier of the food pyramid but for the influence of wheat and corn producers? Why else would milk be considered a food group, but for the influence of the dairy industry?

A recent book on the subject sums it up: *Death by Food Pyramid: How Shoddy Science, Sketchy Politics and Shady Special Interests Ruined Your Health…. and How to Reclaim It* (Denise Minger, 2014).

Many institutions and nutritionists are now offering their own versions of food pyramids and plates. What follows is a sampling of how food pyramids have evolved.

Official US Department of Agriculture Food Guides

1992 Original Food Pyramid

Food Guide Pyramid
A Guide to Daily Food Choices

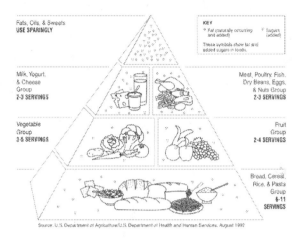

Use the Food Guide Pyramid to help you eat better every day...the Dietary Guidelines way. Start with plenty of Breads, Cereals, Rice, and Pasta; Vegetables; and Fruits. Add two to three servings from the Milk group and two to three servings from the Meat group.

Each of these food groups provides some, but not all, of the nutrients you need. No one food group is more important than another — for good health you need them all. Go easy on fats, oils, and sweets, the foods in the small tip of the Pyramid.

Current Food Plate

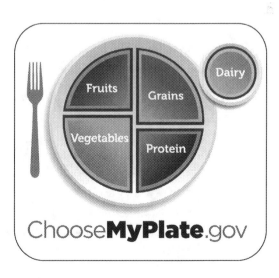

Vegetarian Food Pyramid

Vegetarians live longer and are seldom overweight. Many use vegetarian diets as part of their recovery from surgery and illnesses. Vegetarianism is more sustainable, better for the planet, and clearly more humane. Some Vegetarians suffer from anemia and other frailties. I prefer a modified vegetarian diet to include occasional consumption of wild fish and humanely raised poultry.

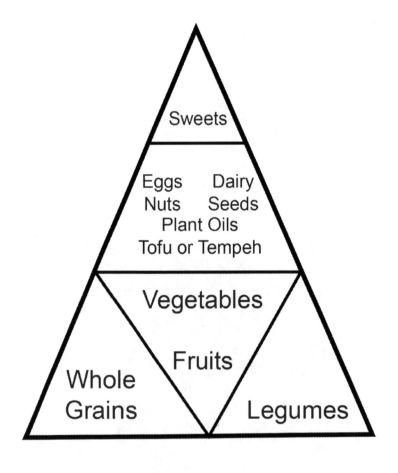

Traditional/Omnivore Food Pyramid

This dietary theory recommends that humanely–raised animal proteins take the place of grains in forming the base of the pyramid. Vegetables follow close behind. Fruits are considered moderation foods and are no longer grouped with vegetables. The prominence of animal fats in this way of eating is controversial.

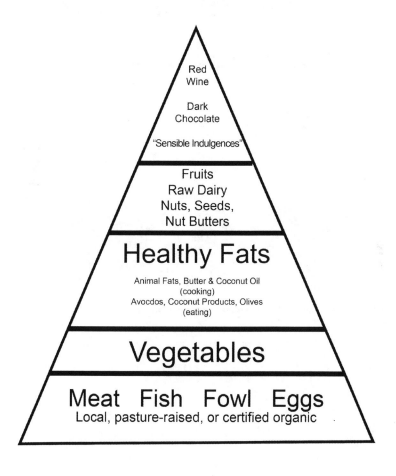

Red
Wine

Dark
Chocolate

"Sensible Indulgences"

Fruits
Raw Dairy
Nuts, Seeds,
Nut Butters

Healthy Fats

Animal Fats, Butter & Coconut Oil
(cooking)
Avocdos, Coconut Products, Olives
(eating)

Vegetables

Meat Fish Fowl Eggs
Local, pasture-raised, or certified organic

Weight Loss "Trapezoid"

*Substitute water for grains and eliminate the
top tier of the original food pyramid*

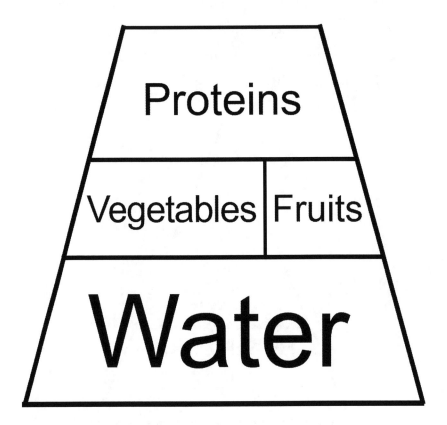

Now it's your turn. If you were to design your own "Best Foods List" and then translate that to a pyramid, what would it look like?

Design Your Own Food Pyramid Process:

1. Make *two* copies of the blank template, provided on page: 74.
2. On the first copied template, enter foods that depict your current diet (*Example:* "My husband's current Food Pyramid")
3. Create a list of the foods you think would be best for you to eat on the provided "10 Best Foods for Me" form. *Be centered and focused before you do this. Breathe.*
4. Enter these foods on the second copied Food Pyramid Template.

Your food list and personal pyramid will change over time. For instance, if you need to drop a few pounds, your food "trapezoid" will change after you have achieved your goal. If you want to try the FODMAP diet for digestive distress, you can discontinue it after it works. If you have a tendency toward weight gain or SIBO (small intestinal bacterial overgrowth), you may want to continue to follow a slightly liberalized variation of these plans.

Sample Personal Food Plan

This Food Pyramid depicts my husband's current eating habits. It should be noted that although he has slightly elevated cholesterol, he is not overweight and he exercises regularly.

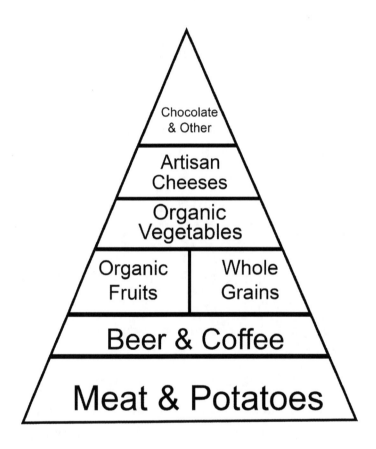

The 10 Best Foods for Me

Be centered and rested before you complete this list.
Consider your heritage, your anatomy, your preferences, and
any conditions you have that may require a special diet.

1.

2.

3.

4.

5.

6.

7.

8.

9.

10.

My Food Pyramid Worksheet

Draw a food pyramid that reflects *how you eat now.*
Then take your "Best Foods for Me List" and
draw a second pyramid that reflects how you *wish*
you would eat. Feel free to add vertical lines.

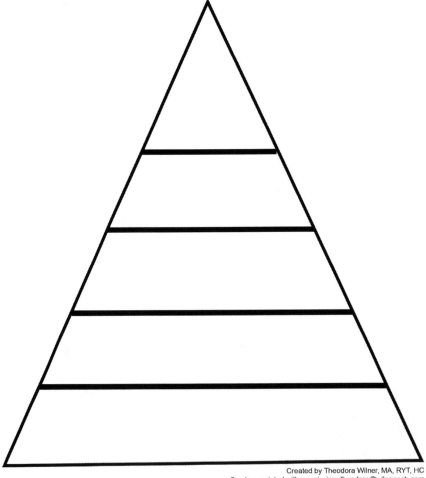

Created by Theodora Wilner, MA, RYT, HC
Can be reprinted with permission: theodora@wilnerweb.com

PART II

SLEEP

This section is about where and how you spend one-third of your life.

Sleep is essential for your physical health. Heart rate and respiration slow down and blood pressure declines during deep sleep, believed to be the most physically restorative time for the body. 80% of human growth hormone is released during sleep. Adequate sleep plays a vital role in helping your body recover from illness and injury.

Sleep is also essential for your mental health. A good night's sleep increases your ability to concentrate, remember (especially short term), handle complex tasks, think logically, assimilate and analyze new information, think critically, communicate clearly and make decisions

In this chapter, you will learn twelve tips for ensuring a better night's sleep, and nine causes of fatigue.

I will also share my own experience with insomnia.

Chapter 12

TO SLEEP, PERCHANCE TO DREAM

It is estimated that a quarter of Americans do not sleep well. Inadequate sleep significantly alters mood, increases depression, lowers the threshold of anger, and increases stress, anxiety, worry, and frustration.

Gallup interviewed over 7,000 adults in 2014 to assess their overall well-being. In this index, those who slept seven hours per night scored higher in the well-being scale than those who slept less.

Hours of sleep required

On average, Americans are getting about one hour less sleep a night than they did in the 1940s. Four out of ten adults fall short of the recommended amount of sleep. (*Gallup poll, 2014*)

Not everyone needs the same amount of sleep. Thomas Edison only needed three to four hours of sleep a night. Bill Clinton only needs four to five hours of sleep a night. Albert Einstein and Calvin Coolidge, on the other hand, preferred to get ten hours of sleep each night.

You can assess your own sleep needs during a relaxing vacation without excessive alcohol or other substances. Go to sleep and wake up anytime you want, without an alarm. Log the hours you sleep each night. After a few nights, you will fall into a pattern of consistency. Note this. This is your sleep need.

Following is a sleep test and twelve tips for getting a good night's sleep. If, after implementing these practices, you still have trouble sleeping, you may want to consult a physician who may refer you for a sleep study. This is a painless overnight in a sleep facility. A sleep technologist records brain activity, heart rhythm, breathing, eye movement, and other biological functions through electrodes and monitors placed on your head, chest, and legs. The data gleaned from this sleep study are tabulated and sent to a physician for analysis. Depending on the results, you will be offered treatments such as oxygen, medication, or a CPAP (continuous positive airway pressure) machine.

Take this Sleep Test _now_

Have you experienced any of these sleep problems?

YES NO   Inability to fall asleep

YES NO   Arouse repeatedly/sleep is light and fragmented

YES NO   Wake up too early/can't return to sleep

YES NO   Snoring or snorting

YES NO   Restless or active legs at night

YES NO   Excessive sleepiness/fatigue during the day

YES NO   Confusion while driving

YES NO   Episodes of impaired awareness

YES NO   Sleep-related near misses or accidents

If you answered YES to two or more of these experiences, you might consider getting a complete sleep evaluation. Meet with your physician who will want to run tests to rule out medical conditions that affect sleep.

12 tips for getting a good night sleep

1. Maintain a regular sleep schedule.

2. Go to bed and wake up at the same time every day, even on weekends and holidays. Somewhere between 10 pm and 6 am is optimal.

3. Honor your natural biorhythm. Before electricity, our ancestors went to bed at sunset and awakened at sunrise. This meant, like hibernating animals, humans slept more in winter when the days were shorter.

4. Avoid drinking alcohol within two hours of bedtime; alcohol disrupts the natural rhythm of your sleep cycles.

5. Eat a light meal in the evening and stop eating two hours before bedtime. Eating a heavy meal in the evening can make sleeping difficult. Eating too fast puts air into the stomach and can cause heartburn. Tomato products and spicy food can cause heartburn, which gets worse when you lie down.

6. Reduce all beverages before bedtime if getting up to urinate disturbs your sleep.

7. Relax! Having a relaxing before-bed ritual can help you fall asleep more quickly
    *   Listen to soothing music
    *   Read a book
    *   Meditate or pray
    *   Soak in a warm bath
    *   Do some relaxing stretches/ yoga poses

8. Create a quality sleeping environment

- Quiet (ear plugs, fan, white noise machine)
- Dark (curtains, eye pillow or eye-shade)
- Cool (65 degrees or less)

9. Discontinue your use of computers, mp3players, cell phones, and TV at least one hour before bed. The glow from these electronics delays the release of melatonin, a sleep-inducing hormone. These devices also stimulate the brain cells, which is the opposite of what you need before sleep.

10. If you awaken in the middle of the night, get out of bed, rather than tossing and turning or lying awake. Read (nothing too stimulating), chant, meditate, or breathe deeply. No paying bills or watching TV.

11. Don't watch the clock. If you find yourself rolling over to check the time every hour, covering your clock may help you sleep better.

12. Use your bed only for sleeping and sex.

Chapter 13

OTHER CAUSES OF FATIGUE

There are other reasons besides sleeplessness that cause us to be tired.

When we get home from work, most of us face another full time job, which may include cooking, cleaning, paying bills and/or minding the children.

After a long hard day, we reward our wearied body and mind with a glass of wine or a cold beer or a big meal topped off with something sweet. Then, we spend a few hours in front of the TV or computer. Sometimes, we lose ourselves in these hypnotic electronics and go to sleep too late, often agitated from the stimulus that preceded it.

Some of these stressors are unavoidable (tending to the children) and you just have to have patience as you grow through it. Some of them *are* avoidable (electronic addiction) and you will do yourself a big favor to modify these habits.

There are also some verifiable medical conditions that cause fatigue. Following are a few of the more common conditions that cause fatigue:

1. **Anemia** — the most common blood disorder.
2. **Chronic pain** — The American Chronic Pain Association estimates that one in three Americans

(approximately 50 million people) suffers from some chronic pain.

3. **Digestive distress** — Most people have some digestive incompetence. Functional physicians and nutritionists believe the root of most imbalance starts in the gut.

4. **Hormonal changes** — e.g., pregnancy, PMS, menopause, birth control pills, impotence.

5. **Infection** — e.g., viral, bacterial, yeast, parasitic or fungal. Often undiagnosed.

6. **Illness or injury** — These require rest. Many people continue to work or return to work before the body is ready.

7. **Low thyroid function** — High carbohydrate diets and gluten place a drag on the thyroid. Often undiagnosed.

8. **"Vague" complaints** — There are numerous conditions for which conventional Western medical practice has no response; e.g., backaches, chronic fatigue or pain.

9. **Side effects from medications** — Over 150 pharmaceuticals list "fatigue or drowsiness" as a side effect.

Chapter 14

INSOMNIA

Insomnia is the inability to obtain an adequate amount or quality of sleep. The difficulty can be in falling asleep, remaining asleep, or both. People with insomnia do not feel refreshed when they wake up.

Insomnia is not a disease — it is a common symptom affecting millions of people that may be caused by many conditions, diseases, or circumstances.

I have insomnia but I practice some remedies that allow me to sleep through most nights. I now have an established bedtime routine that includes relaxation techniques, rituals, and a plethora of sleep aids.

Addressing insomnia is very personal. You'll need to play around with the remedies and see what works for you. For instance, some people can drink coffee into the evening. If I do caffeine – coffee, green tea, or chocolate – I know that 3:00pm is my absolute cut off point. Even that is risky. I prefer to discontinue all forms of caffeine by noon. I only have caffeine later if I'm going out for the evening. When I have chocolate after dark, I pay for it later with insomnia.

My kind of insomnia is the kind where I wake up in the middle of the night. When I do not have too much on my mind, I am able to fall back asleep. When I am very busy, with too much on my plate, I wake up and start thinking, thinking, thinking. This still happens occasionally. I am now prepared for this possibility with guided imagery programs on my iPad which I keep on the floor by my bed. Ear buds are draped over my headboard for easy access in the dark. Listening to relaxing music or guided imagery scripts, is an exception to the rule to avoid electronics at bedtime (from Chapter 12.) I also have a headlight nearby that allows me to read myself back to sleep without disturbing my husband.

Sleeping well depends on the kind of day I've had. Vigorous exercise in the morning and minimal stress during the day are pre-requisites for peaceful sleep.

Before I go to bed, I pay attention to many of the tips listed on p 80-81. I avoid spicy foods at dinner and I don't eat two hours before bed. I reduce my water intake after 6:00 to avoid the possibility of getting up too often to urinate.

No matter what time I go to bed, I seem to wake up at around 6:00-7:00, so it behooves me to have lights out by 11:00-Midnight to get my requisite seven hours of sleep. To have lights out at 11:00, I need to disconnect from the TV or computer by 10:00, and I need to stop eating by 8:00.

Before getting into bed, I reach for the ceiling and then touch my toes. When I get into bed, I turn my toes toward each other to crack my lower back, scrunch my shoulders to my ears, then down my back. Often, I read. After I turn out the light, I do some deep breathing. Inhale deeply. Exhale slowly. *Zzzzzzz.*

Sometimes, especially if I have gone many nights in a row with restless sleep, I'll take a sleep aid. I often use herbs and supplements to ensure a full night's sleep. Here are some that work for me:

Herbal teas

One of my favorites is "Nighty Night Tea" by *Traditional Medicinals®*. This is the best sleep-enhancing formula for me. It contains passionflower, chamomile, linden flower, catnip, hops, and a proprietary blend of spearmint, lemon verbena, lemon peel and lemon grass. Others report a preference for "Sleepytime Tea" by *Celestial Seasons ®*and "Bedtime Tea" by *Trader Joes*. I have tried these and more, but I always go back to my "Nighty Night." You must try them all, too, to see what works best for you.

> *Cautionary Note:* If you are unable to get back to sleep in the middle of the night after getting up to urinate, avoid liquids before bedtime.

Calcium and magnesium (1000/500 mg)
Generally associated with bone health, calcium and magnesium have also been found to be associated with deeper, less interrupted sleep.

Melatonin (3 mg)
Melatonin is a hormone that helps control sleep and wake cycles. Natural melatonin levels drop with age. Light affects

how much melatonin your body produces. It is helpful to take melatonin when you travel across time zones.

"Sleep potions"

I have tried many over-the-counter (OTC) health-store sleep combinations, which I call "Sleep Potions." Each has a slightly different formula. Get to know which one works best for you.

Many people like the effect of Valerian, a sedative (related to the tranquilizer "Valium"). It is in many sleep compounds. I personally do not like its effects. The number of OTC sleep potions available to me is limited because so many contain Valerian.

Amino acids

Sometimes, I take amino acids like GABA, 5HTP. When I take Tryptophan, another amino acid, I wake up with a hangover. Get advice from a Nutritionist on these. Read *The Mood Cure* by Julia Ross (2003) to learn the effects of these amino acids on your brain.

Drugs

Sometimes I take an over-the-counter or prescribed sleeping pill if I have not slept well for several nights. Please consult with a functional, naturopathic, or integrative doctor about these. Sleeping pills must be used judiciously. My physician believes that sleep is so important for health and mood, that occasional medication is preferred over the alternative. I am uneasy with their addictive potential, so I do not use these or any of the aforementioned sleep aids (except for the tea and calcium) more than two nights in a row.

An elderly, conservative neighbor friend, who has been unable to sleep for about ten *years*, was beginning to experience significant health consequences from this pattern. He had tried meditation, relaxation exercises, and every sleep remedy known to man. Almost. When I last talked to him, he had finally found relief in one cannabis cookie, one hour before bed. (In California, Marijuana is legal for medical use; I am not suggesting you break the law.)

PART III

SEEK

When we think of the word Seek, we think of looking for something that will make us feel better, that will lift our spirits.

We open this section with an invitation to seek "endarkenment" and we close this section with an invitation to seek pleasure and play.

In this section, I invite you to seek your authentic self, your greater purpose, your raison d'être, and your relationship to the community and the cosmos.

This section also invites you to find your inner wisdom, to offer gratitude, and to practice meditation. Meditation is calming, healing, and moves you to a higher consciousness. In this section, you will be given suggestions from real meditation masters on how to avoid distractions ("Monkey Mind") while you are meditating.

Chapter 15

SEEK THE DARK

O Mighty Source of all that is:
From sorrow, lead us to everlasting joy,
From darkness, lead us to infinite light.
From "A Festival of Light" by Swami Kriyananda

Barbara Brown Taylor suggests that seekers of "enlightenment" must first find "endarkenment." Taylor questions our tendency to associate all that is good with the light and all that is evil with the dark. In her book, *Learning to Walk in the Dark* (2014), Taylor tells us it is through the darkness that we find courage, and it is while we are in the dark that we grow the most.

Just as we need to eat whole foods, so do we need to become whole human beings. To do this, we must confront our suffering, and often this suffering is caused by our "shadow self." The shadow self is that part of us that lies hidden beneath suppressed or unexpressed feelings.

"What you resist, persists."
Carl Jung

Some of us may belong to a rarified minority that emerged unscathed from the challenges of our youth. More than likely, we have found ourselves inexplicably "triggered" by certain people or circumstances. Or maybe we are unhappy in our work, or fatigued, or depressed, or addicted to substances or electronics, or facing premature health challenges.

These desperate circumstances encourage us to uncover and embrace our shadow self. It is not easy work. You have to face everything that makes you feel unworthy, everything you do not like about yourself. It is only by exposing fears and anxieties that you find the peace and happiness you deserve. You will not know the light until you face the dark. [4]

Questions for getting in touch with your shadow self

Explore any of the following questions that resonate with you.

Begin all self-inquiry with a period of quietude.
Sit quietly and breathe deeply from your diaphragm. Meditate.
(Use the techniques offered at the end of this section.)

Visualize yourself in a comfortable, soothing place.
Ask that the guidance you seek come from a
place of truth and higher awareness.
Keep breathing deeply.

1. Identify what aspects of your life you would like to change.
2. a. Make a list of all the ways in which you do not feel good enough. (E.g., I am not thin enough, tall enough, smart enough, rich enough.)
   b. What is underneath these feelings?
3. What advice do you give to others that you wish you would take yourself?

The desired outcome of this exercise is to identify and release
any early wounds or triggers that may be holding you back
from realizing the inner peace that is your birthright.

Inside Out, a brilliant 2015 animated film by Pixar and Disney, gives this idea a delightful spin.

In this movie, we get to see the *Head*quarters (i.e., brain) of a young girl (Riley) with a JOY-filled life until her parents move her across the country at age 11

At Headquarters, we watch five key emotions — *Joy, Sadness, Disgust, Fear, and Anger* — manage Riley's life. The animation is brilliant. Daily actions become color-coded spheres that line the shelves of Headquarters until they are sent to "Core Emotions" or "Long-Term Memories" for storage.

Joy is the leader in this tribe of emotions. *Joy* bends over backward to make sure Riley is happy as much as possible. One day, *Joy* and *Sadness* get lost in Long Term memories, in the Land of Imagination, and in the Train of Thoughts. Riley's life starts running amuck as *Fear, Disgust*, and *Anger* take charge.

The turning point of the film comes when *Joy* observes *Sadness* practicing empathy and making Riley's old imaginary friend feel better. *Joy* asks, "How did you do that?" And *Sadness* says something like, "I don't know; I just understood how he felt."

Joy then realizes *Sadness* is a necessary emotion and is key in helping Riley feel the pain and sadness of leaving her friends, starting a new school, and all the other challenges of a move. We come to realize that *Sadness, Fear,* and *Anger* are not bad emotions. They have their place and must be expressed. Because it is a Disney film, of course, everyone lives happily ever after.

One could not help but wonder what would have happened to Riley if *Joy* and *Sadness* never made it back to headquarters.

What would have happened to Riley with *Fear, Disgust,* and *Anger* in charge? Would her runaway attempt have succeeded? Would she now be in jail? Or a victim of human trafficking? As often as not, this is what really happens to children of poverty, broken homes, misguided parenting, neglect, and abuse. With fear and anger in charge, many peoples' lives can run amuck and often do.

Most of my childhood was spent acting out for attention or crying about almost everything my three older brothers and parents did and said. I felt like a square peg in a round hole. My mother was particularly critical of me. My father was heard to say, "The problem with Theo is that she thinks with her heart, not with her head." I spent much of my young adult life feeling bad and mad and sad.

When I relocated to California in the early 1970s, I engaged a counselor, and found many friends who shared my views and temperament. I never returned to the East Coast.

My mission now is to support people who, like me, wish to reclaim their health, reduce their cravings, and increase their energy. As a Wellness Advisor, Health Coach, and Yoga Instructor, I am now enjoying a career of service that is creatively and psychologically fulfilling. It took me about 20 years to get here.

Theodora Wilner

Parents are blamed, not trained

Most parents do not know how to parent. It was not their intention to deliberately hurt us. They did the best they could. They said things to keep us in line, to make us polite, to give themselves a few moments of peace. Likely, we have internalized many of their offhand remarks and made them a lot more punishing than they were intended. This voice grows up to become our "Inner Critic." It is a voice that says we're not good enough, thin enough, rich enough, successful enough, and on and on.

It is liberating to get to the point where you can forgive your parents for what they got wrong and honor them for what they got right.

"We have met the enemy and he is us."
Cartoonist Walt Kelly, 1971

Chapter 16

SEEK THE LIGHT

*"What lies behind us and what lies before us are
tiny matters compared to what lies within us."*

Oliver Wendell Holmes

The search for purpose and meaning is necessary if you wish to operate from a place of higher awareness.

I believe we all have a need to see our existence in a broader context. We need to value love, kindness, compassion, and generosity. We need to be in touch with our true natures. We need to seek the light.

In so doing, we will come to appreciate the sacredness of life, and know that true joy lies in manifesting our inner wisdom and connecting with our innate bliss.

Some would call this a spiritual practice. Would you? Is spirituality important to you? How spiritual are you?

To find out, you may want to take the quiz "How Spiritual Are You?" that was developed by psychiatrist, C. Robert Cloninger, MD, author of *Feeling Good: The Science of Well-Being.* You can find it on his website: www.anthropedia.org.

It is possible to live a life with purpose and meaning and not be spiritual. My friend Bill, raised in the Jewish faith, is thoroughly agnostic. I adore him. He is a good, loyal, and generous friend who has a keen sense of social justice and has lived a very purposeful and meaningful life. I would not want to alienate him or anyone like him who would find spirituality to be akin to religiosity which he would think of as the "opiate of the masses."

I, however, am very spiritual. My spirituality is a mixed-up hybrid of many influences.

- I am of Jewish heritage. From these roots, I developed an ingrained devotion to family, education, social justice, and freedom. I did not, however, develop a connection with a personal God.

- Because of my father's fervent belief in education, my three brothers and I were sent to the best schools in Washington DC at that time: As students of St. Albans and National Cathedral School for Girls, we attended Episcopal services at the Washington National Cathedral. I was enchanted by the pageantry and ritual. [5]

- From my Twelve Step Experience (Overeaters Anonymous), I learned that I could define my higher power any way I wanted and turn all my problems over to him/her. And so I did. I developed a belief in a personal higher power and I call her by many names: "God," "Divine Mother," "Great Spirit," and "Mama Guide," to name a few.

- My husband was raised a Baptist; we have found commonality in Buddhism and Eastern–based practices.

YOGA

"Yoga is the yoke that unites the seeker with the sought."

-*Rumi*

The spiritual path that best defines and guides me is YOGA. YOGA is not a religion but it is an ancient spiritual practice on which many religions are based. I practice four kinds of YOGA:

- *Hatha* YOGA: the YOGA of bodily mastery through postures and breathing;
- *Jnana* YOGA: the YOGA of wisdom and knowledge that asks us to lead an examined life. Here we learn to practice "Witness Consciousness" (detachment) and "Self-Inquiry" around issues like desire, judgment, criticism, service, control, triggers, shame, and fear;
- *Karma* YOGA: the YOGA of selfless service; and
- *Raja* YOGA. Also known as "Royal" yoga or the 8-Fold Path, *Raja* YOGA asks us to follow certain codes of behavior (Yamas and NIyamas) like "non-violence," to practice *Hatha* YOGA (*Asana and Pranayama*), and to meditate deeply and regularly through four levels of consciousness (*Pratyahara, Dharana, Diyana and Samadhi*).

Central to YOGA philosophy is a system of "Chakras." These wheel-like vortices of energy housed along the spine, form the basis of our psycho-spiritual nature. Each of these seven chakras or energy centers of consciousness has a different purpose and meaning. They help us understand our mental tendencies, habits, and desires. YOGA and other wellness practices open the chakras. Unhealthy habits and negative thought patterns close them down. For a current and persuasive understanding of the chakras, read books by Carolyn Myss (e.g., *Energy Anatomy* and *Anatomy of the Spirit; The Seven Stages of Power and Healing)*.

If you do not like YOGA, try Chi Gong, Tai Chi, or Feldenkrais. These are similar practices for improving functioning and awakening energy. Of course, you do not need to practice any of these systems to be spiritual nor do you need to be spiritual to be well. You just need to be committed to living a fulfilling, purposeful life.

Chapter 17

PRACTICE GRATITUDE

"Some people grumble because rose bushes have thorns;
I am thankful that thorn bushes have roses."

Alphonse Karr

My spirituality is intimately related to my level of gratitude. I have found gratitude to be the most healing habit I have ever practiced.

For about a year, I kept a journal following the template offered by author Julia Cameron's "Morning Pages" (from *The Artist's Way*, 1992). One of the things Cameron asks you to do in this early morning writing exercise is to list "Ten things you are grateful for that happened yesterday."

I had trouble coming up with ten things every single day. I doggedly complied with the exercise in spite of my resistance.

Then the season changed. I started noticing flowers. And aromas. And colors. And the buzzing of bees and chirping of the birds. They made me smile. Other people were smiling too. I started feeling grateful for our world and the people in it. My gratitude list expanded: Sunshine, daffodils, walking in nature, feeding the ducks, eating on the deck, wearing sandals, the thirst-quenching taste of water, outdoor concerts, riding in the car with the sunroof open, hearing a great radio interview, strawberries, laughing with a friend, reading a happy human interest story, sleeping through the night.

This experience was transformative.

"Gratitude is not only the greatest of virtues,
but the parent of all others."
Cicero, 106-43 BCE

Studies have verified gratitude's effect on body chemistry and the neurological network. In "The Grateful Brain: the neuroscience of giving thanks" (*Psychology Today*, November 2012), several studies show how gratitude can help you sleep better and be happier.

In one study, (Ng *et al.*, 20 12) a group of researchers looked at the effects of gratitude and sleep on symptoms of depression. Higher levels of gratitude were associated with better sleep and with lower anxiety and depression. Regardless of their levels of insomnia, people who showed more gratitude were less depressed.

In another study, NIH (National Institutes of Health) researchers examined the blood flow in various brain regions while subjects summoned up feelings of gratitude (Zahn *et al.*, 2009). Subjects who showed more gratitude had higher levels of activity in the hypothalamus. The hypothalamus controls a huge array of essential bodily functions, including eating, drinking, and sleeping. It also has a huge influence on your metabolism and stress levels.

The practice of gratitude has even been found to have a positive effect on our genes. Just the thought of gratitude translates into beneficial biochemical and neurological changes in your body. Gratitude also has the effect of dissolving old resentments and grievances.

Finally, gratitude has an expansive effect. When you express gratitude to another person, you are transmitting those same physiological and mental benefits to that person. Could it be that gratitude is the secret weapon for harmonizing the world?

Chapter 18

BUDDHIST MIND-TRAINING PRACTICES

Buddhism offers 59 mind-training ("Lojong") slogans for transcending ego and awakening to the light of your true nature. Following are some of my favorites:

These are short and self-explanatory:

- Be grateful to everyone
- Always maintain a joyful mind
- Abandon poisonous food
- Don't be so predictable
- Don't malign others
- Don't always try to be the fastest
- Always meditate on whatever provokes resentment
- Don't expect applause

These require a little explanation:

Transform all mishaps into the path

The obstacles that confound us are also our means for awakening. You can welcome them into your life rather than avoiding them, waiting for them to pass, or denying their existence. This does not mean that we will necessarily overcome all our problems. It means that we can accept all things, good and bad.

All activities should be done with one intention

We are overwhelmed by obligations and worries about survival, appreciation, and success. It would be better if your words, thoughts, and emotions were expressions of one intention— to benefit all sentient beings.

Don't wait in ambush

This one is about the resentful mind, the mind that holds grudges. This unforgiving attitude can cause us to isolate ourselves, to become rigid and to obsess about revenge. This is a pattern that victimizes individuals, organizations, and nations. When we let these attitudes take over our minds, we become slaves to others' actions. We need to free ourselves from this unhealthy pattern.

Don't talk about injured limbs

Do not call attention to those with defects or problems. We are both fascinated and repulsed by others' deformities and weaknesses. View the world and all the people in it with awareness and acceptance.

Change your attitude, but remain natural

Your response to adversity is shaped by your attitude, which is your usual way of thinking about things. Your attitude colors your perspective on everything. Make an effort to care for others as much as you care about yourself. Just get over yourself, and then relax.

Do these sound familiar? They are variations on the Golden Rule

The Golden Rule

Do unto others, as you would have them do unto you.
Christianity

What is hateful to you; do not to your fellow man
Judaism

Hurt not others in ways that you
yourself would find hurtful.
Buddhism

No one of you is a believer until he desires for
his brother that which he desires for himself.
Islam

Chapter 19

MEDITATE

Don't just do something, sit there!
Sylvia Boorstein

Stop. Close your eyes. Relax your body. Breathe.

Wouldn't it be wonderful if these were the instructions you were given upon awakening, before you entered your car, when you arrived at work, and before every class, presentation, test, and meal?

Just close your eyes. Breathe. Relax your body. Relax your mind.

If you received more encouragement to slow down, tap into your right brain, and breathe, you would feel better on multiple levels. You would have less anxiety, frustration and anger and more composure and serenity. You would be more present-centered, more appreciative of every moment. You would be calmer, clearer thinking, and healthier. You would live long and well, and you would die in peace.

These are just a few of the many benefits of meditation.

Meditation is a way to transform the mind. It is a practice of tuning into the deep peace that is inside us. It requires concentration and practice. By focusing inward and calming your mind, you will eventually reach a higher level of awareness.

"Over 380 published, peer-reviewed research studies on the Transcendental Meditation technique have documented its effectiveness for stress-related conditions, brain function, and more."
Transcendental Meditation, a non-profit organization

Documented Benefits of Meditation

- **Reduces** stress, anxiety, insomnia, blood pressure, congestive heart failure, cholesterol stroke, metabolic syndrome, cardiovascular risk, pain, and substance abuse
- **Improves** levels of brain functions, intelligence, creativity, learning ability, school behavior, academic achievement and athletic performance

---

There are many meditation techniques. You can learn how to meditate through YouTube, TV, by reading a book, or through a variety of classes taught in schools, libraries, synagogues, churches, ashrams, yoga centers, Buddhist groups, and recreation centers. Find a meditation class for you that is accessible, affordable and fits your schedule.

I learned meditation as part of my YOGA training at *Ananda,* a global movement based on the teachings of Paramahansa Yogananda. Ananda has retreats, meditation groups, online classes, books, music, and spiritual communities around the world *(www.ananda.org)*

Not always in YOGA classes or studios, but almost always in YOGA retreats and centers, *Hatha* YOGA will be followed by a sitting meditation. *Hatha* YOGA was intended as a first step for discharging tensions and toxins, relaxing the body, and clearing the mind in readiness for meditation.

To this day, I cannot enjoy a fulfilling meditation practice without preceding it with YOGA or some physical movement. You do not need to practice YOGA before meditating, but I highly recommend you move your body in some way beforehand so you can release the stressors that can disrupt your focused attention.

How to Meditate

Step 1. Prepare

Move your body so as to discharge the tensions and toxins that can result in a busy, distracting mind. You may want to start your meditation session with a writing practice to empty your head of distracting thoughts.

Step 2. Perfect Your Posture, Straighten Your Spine

Find a quiet place where you can sit, stand, or lie comfortably. Perfect your alignment. Lift and lengthen your spine. Stack each vertebra upon the one below.

Step 3. Breathe

Breathe consciously from your diaphragm, in and out through your nose if you are not congested. Inhale deeply. Exhale slowly. Repeat until you have a slow undulating rhythm. Practice a Pranayama if you know how to do this. Pranayama is a YOGA practice for activating your "Prana" (life force) through various deep breathing patterns.

Step 4. Focus

Focus on your breath or choose a word, a mantra, or an image from nature, as your point of focus. It is important for you to have a focusing point that you can return to when your mind wanders.

Step 5. Note the Distraction and Let It Go

Should inside mind chatter, outside noises, or physical sensations distract you, just note them, and let them go. Bring your attention back to your breath, your posture, and your point of focus.

Step 6. Closing: Offer Loving Kindness

Conclude your session by transmitting the good energy you've gained through your meditation to your friends and family, the community, the nation, the world. You can just ask to spread good will to soul friends everywhere. Or you can be targeted in directing healing energy to the bodies, minds, and spirits of those you know who are sick or suffering. Often, the newspaper headlines direct me to those I wish to bless.

Closing Blessings

Let us help make the world a place where
Love dominates our hearts,
Nature sets the standard for beauty,
Kindness guides our actions, and
We all awaken to the light of our true nature
Adapted by Theodora Wilner from a poem by Susan Polis Schutz

Let there be love, and light, and peace in the world,
And let it begin with me.
Unity

May all beings have happiness,
May all beings be free from suffering,
May all beings be free of attachment and aversion,
May all beings be free.
Buddhist Metta

May the frightened cease to be afraid,
May those bound be freed,
May the powerless find power,
And may we all benefit one another.
Santideva

"Monkey Mind"

Monkey mind is a Buddhist term that describes a distracted state of mind, a mind that is diverted from its focused intent.

It is a term that applies to the frustrating thoughts and obsessive thinking that we encounter when we would prefer to be emptying our mind of workaday thoughts and encumbrances. It is also a state of mind that most of us experience in spite of our best efforts to keep it at bay.

The frequency and consistency of my monkey mind during meditation motivated me to ask special friend-meditators how they handled monkey mind. I was tired of carving out daily time for inner stillness, only to have that time filled with planning dinner parties and reviewing my to-do lists for the day.

I polled people who I knew had an established meditation practice and asked: "Are you ever victimized by monkey mind during meditation? If yes, how do you deal with it?"

100% of the respondents said "of course" they experienced monkey mind, although few would use the term "victimized." Most of these evolved practitioners simply accepted it for what is.

Interestingly, there was not unanimity in the way they responded to monkey mind when it faced them. Their responses were diversified and useful and made me want to share this wisdom. I believe their suggestions form the basis of a practical meditation practice.

Tips from Meditation Masters

On preparing

"Preparation before sitting makes all the difference so that I may befriend my own mind. I write down any roving thoughts or to do's so that there'll be less interference. Then I engage in several yoga asanas (postures); then universal prayers for family, friends, and all people; then breathing exercises. Then I sit on my cushion and offer light, incense and ring the bell to all incarnations and great ones of the past, the present and to come."

Mary T

At the Chopra Center last year, we always began meditation with 3 questions, which set the intention and space for the meditation, and I found these to be useful: Who am I? What do I really want? What is my purpose?

Max

Don't go into meditation with any idea of accomplishment or intention for that session. The practice is ever-new and full of surprises. If we try to control the process we block whatever might want to happen. Personally, when I go into meditation, I just say, "I love you God, and I am just sitting here to spend some time with you."

Bhavani

On Breathing

Meditation happens when I get rid of all outside distraction and begin slow and steady breathing. I think about my diaphragm as I say In and Out.

If thoughts distract me, I go back to the breathing pattern. After around 20 minutes or so, my brain believes I am serious and starts to relax.

Jane C

On Point of Focus

"Hong Sau" is a 5 thousand year old mantra that has been given to us for defeating the wandering mind.

Ananta

I use a technique called Centering Prayer. My intention is crystallized in a word that reminds me of my desire to detach. This word doesn't function as any kind of mantra. It is, rather, a simple reminder not to resist nor retain the thought, but to let go in a "receptive" fashion. When I realize I am caught in thinking, I remember my word (and my intention) and release the thought.

Ray

For me, distraction is just lack of a one pointed focus. If it's a line of thinking I can't seem to get out of, I put my guru in front of me and give it to him. If it's just random stuff that keeps popping up, then I focus really hard at the point between the eyebrows and do a few "kriyas" or "hong-sau." (Author's note: meditation techniques)

Matt

Usually my eyes (hence concentration and focus) have drifted to the subconscious (by looking or sinking down into the past) or into the conscious (I am looking straight ahead planning my day, thinking about what someone said...). So I first come back to the breath and refocus my attention at the spiritual eye, feeling as though I am offering all that I am, all my heart, mind, and soul into the hands of the Divine Infinite.

Sabari

I call on my guru when I "finally" notice that I am somewhere other than in the present. I look at him, visualize him, talk to him, try to feel his presence and love and desperately call to him to be with me and help me to be able to do what he has given me to do.

Maria

Refocusing the eyes at the point between the eyebrows, to re-enter the super conscious state can break the wandering state.

Ananta

On Getting Distracted

I get distracted almost every time. I start with a few deep breaths. I try to return to my mantra. And I try not to worry about it! Sometimes more successfully than others. But even when I'm not terribly successful, I find the time meditating to be helpful.

Barbara

The problem of getting distracted during meditation is the ongoing challenge to everyone's practice. Over years of meditating we learn to hold our concentration successfully for longer and longer periods of time, but we all eventually get distracted. I would say to a student "don't be so hard on yourself when you lose your concentration." One must be patient - training the mind to single-pointed focus is a life-long process.

Bhavani

For me, it is all about attitude towards thoughts, and my intention about what to do about thoughts. I do <u>not</u> believe I can stop my mind and the thoughts that arise from my mind. I do think, and know, that I can <u>detach</u> from the thoughts and set my intention to do so. Simple to say, a lifetime to do.

Ray

It is always good to remember that the mind does wander, especially in very intelligent people as there is a load of mental creative energy, so don't feel as if you're the only one who is battling this.

Ananta

"I believe that thoughts are very needy. They will exist only if paid attention to. If I treat my mind as a living room and simply watch the thoughts as they enter through the front door without getting carried away by the thought, they will not stay long. This will prevent the usual process of thought leading to other thoughts, thereby reducing the number of thoughts and allow me the appreciation of the space between

thoughts. At some point this space will become long enough to be called "Samadhi."

Name withheld by request

I use guided imagery recordings a lot when I meditate, so my goal is always to come back to the guided voice that I am listening to - having that as a place of grounding is very useful for me.

Max

Walking meditation

For those of you who have trouble sitting for long periods of time, walking meditation may be just the thing for you.

Walking meditation is about walking slowly and mindfully. You are walking to walk. You are not walking to get somewhere or get more steps on your Fit bit or beat your speed record or burn off calories. This is not an aerobic walk.

A recent study, reported by Gretchen Reynolds in the *New York Times* on July 22, 2014, found that walking outside not only calms the mind, but also can "change the working of our brains in ways that improve our mental health."

A study coordinated by Gregory Bratman, a graduate student at Stanford University, found that "volunteers who walked briefly through a lush, green portion of the Stanford campus were more attentive and happier afterward than volunteers who strolled for the same amount of time near heavy traffic."

Walking Meditation Technique

"When you practice walking meditation, you go for a stroll.
You have no purpose or direction in space or time.
The purpose of walking meditation is walking meditation itself.
Going is important, not arriving."
A Guide to Walking Meditation by Thich Nhat Hanh

Start by "dissecting" your step. Slowly pick up your foot, and place it down before you lift your other foot for the next step. Do it again. Consciously. Name the actions that are involved in a step. Here is how you might describe one step:

- Lift *(the heel)*
- Move *(the foot forward)*
- Place *(the foot down on the ground in front of you)*
- Shift *(your weight to the front of the foot as you lift the other heel)*
- Repeat with the other foot

Repeat this mantra to accompany your steps as you walk very slowly.

Lift → Move → Place → Shift

Breathe and Smile

Match your steps to the breath. Inhale on the "Lift and Move" then Exhale on the "Place and Shift." Let yourself smile. Thich Nhat Hanh speaks of the "Half Smile" where you curl up the corners of your mouth and retain that half smile throughout your walk. When you walk outside, you will find yourself smiling at the trees, the birds, the clouds, and the sky. Let the smile become you.

Blessing

Once you have mastered the slow mindful walk, you will find yourself walking rhythmically. You may then wish to synch your steps with a blessing.

My favorite:

> I touch the earth, the earth touches me.
> I love the earth, the earth loves me.
> I bless the earth, the earth blesses me.
> I am the earth, the earth is me.

> *Adapted from Native American wisdom and*
> *I Touch the Earth, the Earth Touches me by Hugh Prather*

Chapter 20

SEEK JOY

In one of his free 21-day meditation experiences (with Oprah Winfrey,) Deepak Chopra asks us, "What is the meaning of Life?"

"With a serious expression, we expect a deep answer to this question," Chopra says. "But what if we live in a Recreational Universe?"

He goes on to tell us about "Lila," a Sanskrit word that means "the play of creation." Creation is said to arise from a sense of playfulness and enjoyment, not to carry out some deep, serious purpose invented by the mind.

"This may come as a shock," Deepak acknowledges, since there are so many moments when we feel "trapped by things we must do, opinions we must hold, and a path we must follow."

Too often, life is heavy. We are filled with worries and fears. But being too serious can smother our joyfulness and keep our spirits down.

Play and pleasure are vital, yet often neglected aspects of a wellness lifestyle. They allow the left brain to rest. They release stress, liberate blocked thoughts, and stimulate energy. They prompt positive thinking.

Recently, I have re-discovered a love of free form dancing and Zumba. This, in spite of having been kicked out of the

Washington School of Ballet when I was ten. I think I always loved to dance, but was slightly scarred by this ballet trauma.

When we become adults, we fall into a cultural bias that scorns pleasure and play. Of greater import, we are told, is our obligation to family and work. But we become imbalanced when we put others before ourselves most of the time and do not seek activities that restore our energy, revitalize our spirit, and make us feel good.

Playfulness is a casualty of adulthood. It is time to get it back.

Do this exercise to identify what gives you pleasure.

10 Things I Love to Do

1.

2.

3.

4.

5.

6.

7.

8.

9.

10.

*Next to each item, write the day, month, or year
when you last enjoyed this activity.
How long has it been since you have participated in activities
that are fun or give you pleasure?*

*Plan to do some of these long, lost pleasures this coming month.
Circle these.*

Chapter 21

SERVICE

"Be the change you wish to see in the world."

Mahatma Gandhi

Tikkun olam is a Jewish tradition for contributing what you can for the betterment of humanity. The phrase means "healing the world." Philanthropy, charitable giving, and volunteerism go way back in my family history. My maternal grandfather, a Jewish immigrant from Russia, built a men's clothing empire in Canada called *Tip Top Tailors*. His wife used his fortune to support the formation of Israel, host fundraisers, create a summer camp, and numerous other charities. My paternal grandfather, also a Jewish immigrant who spoke four languages, pursued a law degree in night school, sat on many boards and commissions, and was the president of *Adas Israel* Congregation in Washington, D.C. for 25 years. My father and mother inherited their parents' social consciousness and generosity and modeled it to us children.

Service is central to Christian theology. The story of Jesus washing the feet of his disciples at the Last Supper is legendary. "Now that I have washed your feet," Jesus says, "so should you wash one another's feet. I have set you an example that you should do as I have done."

In "Service to Mankind is the Essence of Islam," (Ahmadiyya Gazette, 1999), author Nasim Rehmatullah describes the Muslim practice of giving as "love for humanity, kindness in our hearts for others, a charitable disposition, humility, honesty, a desire to share knowledge with others, and a constant desire to strive by doing good."

Other religions share this devotion to helping and healing. *Seva* is a Sanskrit word which means "selfless service." It describes work that is done without any expectation of reward or repayment. This practice is common to Hindus, Buddhists, Sikhs, and others.

Although religion, social service, and charity go hand in hand, you need not be religious to be generous of time and talent. We are always hearing stories of ordinary humans performing good deeds, like the neighbor who rescues the cat from the tree, the fire fighter who saves the child from a burning house, and the three Sacramento heroes who stop the terrorist on the Paris train. Ordinary people collect trash from our streets, build homes for the disabled, help hospitalized children, donate food to the homeless, and send clothes to victims of natural disasters. Kudos to those of you who have participated in these random acts of kindness.

Children are innately kind. Keep this natural instinct by encouraging generous behavior. When my daughters were young, we came up with a formula for their allowance: "Spend, Save, and Share." It is a lesson they have never forgotten. To this day, we receive about a dozen calendars (solicitations) from charitable organizations (mostly nature and wildlife causes) that my daughter began donating to when she was about eight years old.

Service is not just about doing, it is about being. Live in harmony with yourself, with other people, and with the land around you. The more you practice the ways of wellness, the more energy you will have to be kind and giving to those around you. Be helpful. Spread love. Lighten your carbon footprint. Smile.

"Practice Random Kindness and other Senseless Acts of Beauty"

Anne Herbert

PART IV

STRIDE

The word STRIDE has three, glorious meanings:

1. To walk with long steps;
2. To cope easily and without undue effort or hesitation as in to "take things in stride;" and
3. To take a step forward, to reach one's highest level of efficiency as in to "hit one's stride."

This section will look at each of these three concepts.

When you hit your stride, you will probably be practicing a higher level of wellness than you did before. This is the culmination of our journey.

Chapter 22

WALKING AND MORE

Striding (walking, hiking, or running) is one component of an optimal physical fitness program.

For those of you who are sedentary or have never been much for exercise, walking is a simple, free way to get started. It is suitable for all ages, sizes, and fitness levels, and has many benefits:

- Lowers blood pressure
- Relieves insomnia
- Increases "good" (HDL) cholesterol
- Prevents diabetes
- Improves strength and muscle tone
- Stimulates the mind
- Facilitates weight loss
- Relieves stress and tension
- Reduces the risk of colon cancer
- Reduces body fat
- Builds stronger bones
- Reduces feelings of depression and anxiety

"I'm too tired" is a common excuse for not exercising. Ironically, exercise gives you more energy and pep. So, if you can find ways to fit it in, you'll be less tired. If you've chosen to start your walking practice with 30 minutes a day, try skipping one half hour of TV at night. Walk right after dinner before you sit down to watch TV. You will sleep better that night for having done so. Or split your walk; walk a bit before work, during your lunch hour, and after dinner.

"I don't have enough time in my day to exercise" is another common excuse for not doing so. Look at the "1440" chart to get a better perspective of how much time 60 minutes of walking would take out of your day. These 60 minutes do not need to be done all at one time.

To keep things interesting, vary your route, walk with a friend, or listen to your favorite upbeat music or podcasts.

Or get a dog. A tired dog is a happy dog owner. My Golden Retriever died a few years ago, but when he was alive, we would walk every morning, rain or shine. It was never a burden. I'd just roll out of bed, grab my walking clothes off the bathroom hook, and head out the door. I am lucky that my suburban home borders a 400-acre county park near the American River, so the walk was a beautiful one. Few people were awake in the early morning hours, so Kipper could run off the leash. True to his breed, Kipper had a people-loving temperament. He would always look back to make sure I was okay, greet passers-by with a wagging tail, and come when called. I sure miss him. And my walking is now half of what it was before. I need a dog.

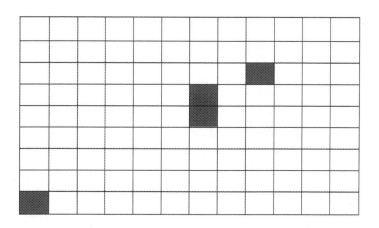

"60/1440"
Thare are 1,440 minutes in a 24-hour day.
This chart represents one day, divided into 15-minute increments.
The blackened squares represent 60 minutes of exercise.
You can do it!

The best exercise is the one you'll do

For forever and a day, this has been my motto.

Forget the charts and articles that tell you how much and how often to walk, how high to sustain a designated heart rate, how far and fast to go, or how much you need to sweat. On the other hand, if you are someone who needs to be challenged, by all means add some healthy competition with yourself or others.

How you move your body is up to you. Just be sure you're doing *something*. You have a better chance of maintaining an exercise program if you have chosen something that you love to do, that is close to home, that fits into your schedule, and that is free or low cost.

I have a friend who danced herself thin through dance videos. I have another friend who, at age 50, enrolled in a tap dancing class. There are many classes for active older adults – chair yoga, "silver stretch and tone," arthritis water classes, and Zumba Gold.

Just do *something*. Being a couch potato, being sedentary, will lead to countless health problems. With inactivity, your muscles will atrophy, your joints will ache, your weight will climb, your heart will weaken, and you will die a slow and painful death.

Benefits of Exercise

Increase energy levels
Increase aerobic capacity

Build self-esteem
Build muscle mass

Add years to your life
Add life to your years

Strengthen bones
Strengthen heart

Promote good posture
Promote healthy aging

Reduce anxiety/stress
Reduce body fat

Control blood pressure
Control appetite

Improve sleep quality
Remove fatigue

Decrease depression
Increase happiness

Chapter 23

THE OPTIMAL PHYSICAL FITNESS PROGRAM

There are eight movements required for an optimal physical fitness program. These should be practiced daily.

- Bend
- Balance
- Pull
- Push
- Squat
- Stride
- Lunge
- Twist

Here is a five-minute sequence that includes all of the above:

- **Bend —**
  Bend forward toward your toes, but don't worry about touching your toes. Bend your knees if you have a bad back. Hang loosely, like a Raggedy Ann doll, dangling your head, arms, and shoulders.

- **Balance —**
  Stand on one foot. Then the other.

- **Pull —**

  Pretend like your pulling weights toward you. Extend your arms out in front of you, palms *up.* Bend at the elbows, pulling your palms *toward you* while contracting your biceps, those muscles at the top of your upper arms.

- **Push —**

  Pretend like your pushing weights away from you. Extend your arms in front of you, palms *down.* Bend at the elbows; pull your forearms, knuckles of the hands toward you. Then push your palms *away from you* while contracting your triceps, the muscles in the back of the upper arms. You could also hold your arms straight out to a wall with your body on an incline, feet about two feet from the wall. Then do "Push Ups" on the wall.

- **Lunge —**

  Bend front leg and extend your other leg straight back, about hip distance from your other leg. Make sure your feet are both facing forward. Then reverse legs. You can do this against a wall for added support.

- **Twist —**

  Swing your arms from side to side, twisting your torso with the movement. To affect all vertebrae, you can lift your arms higher and higher as you swing, till you reach your shoulders and then lower them again. This will adjust the vertebrae, irrigate the spine, and lubricate the disks.

- **Squat** —

    With knees bent, separate your legs. Bend your knees in a way that does not allow them to come forward of your toes; place your knees over your ankles. Extend your buttocks back. Squat as low as you can. Don't overdo it, especially if you have bad knees. You could also place your back on the wall with feet about 2-3 feet in front of you (depending on your height; distance from wall should be about the length of your femur.) Then slide your back down the wall, only as far as your knees allow. Hold there and breathe.

- **Stride** —

    If you cannot run or walk outside due to weather or an injury, walk or run in place, about 50-100 steps.

Striding is the only one of these eight movements that will *not* be taught in a *Hatha* YOGA class. So if you walk (or run or play tennis or other "striding" activity) *and* practice YOGA, you'll have all the bases covered.

Those of you who are seasoned exercisers will want to vary your routine to include strength, flexibility, and endurance.

And you'll want to change it up seasonally to include different activities, different walking/running/hiking paths, and/or different group exercise teachers. Another word for this is "cross training."

Benefits of *Hatha* YOGA

- Reduces stress
- Improves respiration
- Tones the digestive system; decreases gastrointestinal distress
- Improves the functioning of internal organs
- Balances an unbalanced body
- Massages and revitalizes internal organs
- Increases blood flow; stimulates the release of toxins from the body
- Strengthens muscles and makes them more flexible
- Loosens joints and makes them more supple
- Promotes proper body alignment
- Brings a sense of tranquility to the mind

Join a health and fitness club

STOP! DO NOT SKIP THS SECTION just because you hate gyms.

Just give me a moment of your attention. You can still decide after you've heard my pitch to never, ever, enter a health club.

Health clubs are not just about exercise machines. I do not like these machines much, either. I only do machines when it's dark and the weather is murky and dismal or when I'm taking a circuit training class and the trainer makes me use them. I don't understand why you would choose to walk on a treadmill on a gorgeous day when walking outside would do so much more for your mind and spirit. But who am I to judge? Different strokes for different folks. The best exercise is the one you'll *do*!

Fitness clubs are in every neighborhood. I am guessing there is one in your neighborhood or near your work. There is a club for every budget. There are huge clubs with tennis courts and pools, and there are strip mall circuit training shops like *Curves*. I just peeked into a fitness circuit training storefront the other day called "9Round" that offered a 30-minute kickboxing workout. I watched very sweaty young men and women move around to different stations where they kicked, punched, squatted, and jump-roped their way into fitness.

What I love about fitness clubs are the group exercise classes (aka "Group Ex"). When I moved to a new neighborhood a decade ago, I tried out three different clubs in my neighborhood. I chose *California Family Fitness* because my membership allowed me to go to any of their 19 Sacramento clubs and they had the most group fitness classes and the best instructors. There are four *Cal Fam Fit* clubs within my driving comfort zone, which quadruples the numbers of classes available to me.

This is what I love about group fitness classes:

1. If you join a club where there are many classes, you are sure to find something that's suitable for your age, size and fitness level.
2. You are assured of a responsible workout, because a skilled teacher will start with warm ups, end with a cool down or stretch, and offer modifications for challenging movements in between.
3. There are classes all day long — at 5:30 am and 7 pm for the 9-5:00 working crowd —and late morning, mid-day for those with flexible schedules.
4. There is so much variety in the types of classes that you will never get bored. Here is a partial list of the classes offered at *California Family Fitness:*

- Gentle YOGA
- Mixed levels YOGA
- Family YOGA
- Power YOGA
- Piloga
- Pilates
- Core
- Group Strength Training
- Group Interval Training

- Aqua Aerobics
- X-Bike
- Cycle
- Soccer Power
- Zumba
- Zumba Gold
- Boot Camp
- Tai Chi
- Kickboxing
- Glow Aerobics
- Cardio Dance
- Step
- Advanced Choreography Step
- Silver Sculpt & Stretch
- Hot Hula
- Young at Heart
- Belly Dancing

For a description of these classes and more, go to *www.californiafamilyfitness.com*. Then check out the clubs in *your* area. See how they compare.

What you need to know about group fitness classes is that different teachers will interpret each class differently. There are many different approaches to the same fitness practice. Just because a class is labeled "Gentle YOGA" does not mean that it will feel gentle to you. A 22-year- old YOGA teacher's interpretation of "Gentle" will probably be very different from that of a 52- year-old YOGA teacher. A *Bikram*-trained YOGA teacher will have a different interpretation of "Gentle" than an *Ananda* -trained teacher. [6] If you don't like a class, try another. Try five.

A single instructor will also vary her routine, so that what you get in one class will be very different in the next class. For instance, a Pilates teacher may choose to emphasize gluteus (backside) work in one class, and in the next she may concentrate on abdominals (belly muscles). You will likely prefer one to the other. Don't assume that the first class you attend is the way it will always be.

Also, the class that challenges you is probably the one you need the most, but don't let the difficulty of it keep you away. You will get stronger. It will get easier. I love Zumba Gold classes but am always perplexed and stumbling all over myself when the teacher offers new dances. But once I master the new routine, a sense of achievement is added to the endorphin rush that is inherent in the experience. Plus, the variety keeps me from getting bored.

I ask students to try at least three classes with the same teacher and five classes with multiple teachers before they decide on the best fit.

I am partial to the older, more experienced teachers like myself. We have been around for a while. We know what works and what doesn't. We make you feel normal for needing to modify, rather than deficient.

I have been teaching YOGA for almost 20 years. I can no longer rest my head on the floor in front of me, between my widespread legs. My students seem to feel relieved when I go to the wall for support in balancing poses. Do not shy away from classes because you are older and stiffer and cannot do what you used to do. This is the time when you most need exercise to keep your arthritic joints flexible, to increase strength, to prevent falls through improved balance, and to protect your degenerative back issues with core strengthening.

I have tried many classes and definitely have my preferences. (The following names have been changed to protect the innocent.) For instance, it took me awhile to get beyond Sasha's high-pitched, nasal voice and drill-sergeant mentality. But I came to appreciate her knowledge of Pilates and anatomy. Kelly is one dimensional and repetitive, but her cueing is precise and easy to follow. Conversely, Tom does a terrible job of cuing but his Zumba dance moves are awe-inspiring. Mary has the personality of a milk toast, but she knows her stuff and is particularly good at teaching us how to modify challenging movements. Ginger keeps us moving in aqua aerobics and always reminds us to drink water. Karen has a terrific personality. Ada is semi-skilled in a number of class formats and therefore substitutes for many classes; I make a rapid exit when I see her coming.

OK, thank you for indulging me. If you have not been convinced, feel free to try something else. Make your workout your own. The best exercise is the one you'll do.

My personal fitness plan

Before I tell you what I do to stay fit today, you must know that I was an athlete.

My favorite sport of all time was kickball. That was in sixth grade. After that, I played many team sports, including basketball, softball, and field hockey. I was a badminton doubles champ and a blue ribbon swimmer. I received the Award for "Outstanding Girl Athlete" of my high school class.

I celebrated my 40th birthday with a four-mile run through Santa Monica, California, stopping periodically to engage in the *Parcourse* stations along the way. *Parcourses* were simple strength-building structures built in parks, to enhance the public's physical fitness prowess. They included incline benches, overhead bars, tires, and such.

On one of these stations, I wrenched my back and developed a herniated disk. The recovery was long and painstaking. I was the Director of Government Relations for a trade association at the time; I used to write my correspondence, reports, speeches, and testimonies on my back, on the floor, in my office. My self-prescribed rehabilitation consisted of chiropractic care, massage, physical therapy, alternating heat and ice, and rest. I believe it was the rest that was the most important of these interventions. When I got home after work, two young children notwithstanding, I would spend as much time as feasible on my back in bed. I do not know what I would have done without my energetic and devoted husband.

These interventions saved me from surgery. At the pre-op physical, the day before I was scheduled for surgery, my doc said, "You're better!" and took me off the surgery list. That was the good news. He also told me that bulging disks never fully recover, that my disk would degenerate and collapse over time, and that I should avoid all "ballistic" sports from this point forward. This meant nothing jarring (like running) or stop-and-go (like the racquet ball my husband and I had been enjoying since we met).

I was devastated. My whole persona was assaulted. I could no longer be an athlete.

Flash forward 20 years. The doctor's prophecies were true. X-rays show disk degeneration and I am two inches shorter due to the loss of cushioning in several vertebrae (and from my worsening scoliosis). This has not stopped me from exercising regularly. Today, my fitness plan consists of the following:

Monday and Wednesday –
I teach a one-hour yoga class. Before or after I teach, I take a one hour circuit training or Zumba class in the winter and/or one hour of water aerobics in the summer.

Tuesday –
One-hour Pilates class followed by a one hour-cardio class.

Thursday –
Half-hour walk and then I teach a chair YOGA class. A Zumba or water aerobics class or a massage follows this.

Friday —

One-hour circuit training or YOGA in winter and water aerobics in summer.

Saturday –

One and one half-hour yoga class with my husband followed by a relaxing breakfast out. In summer, we often go kayaking.

Sunday –

One-hour walk or nothing.

+

Anytime, Anywhere I can – I dance!

I wore a Fitbit for a while, and even though some activities did not seem to register, I routinely hit or exceeded the 10, 000 step-a-day benchmark. On vacations, even though I eat whatever I want, I seldom gain weight and often lose weight because of all the walking I do.

This is what my body wants right now, and I am fortunate to have gaps in my consulting work to allow for this much physical activity. If I have a client or appointment that conflicts with any of my group fitness classes, I add an evening stroll. Or I skip a day of activity. I am so confident and comfortable in my exercise practice that I am never worried about missing a day or two if I'm just not up for it or have something else I want to do instead.

Chapter 24

TAKE THINGS IN STRIDE

Another phrase for this concept is "Stress Management."

I have been teaching stress management workshops for years. These classes always fill up. Most people, especially working parents, are stressed out and don't mind admitting it. It is usually because we have to juggle many responsibilities, which leaves little time to care for our own needs. Fatigue, family tensions, tight budgets, and aching backs add additional stress to existing challenges. Are *you* stressed?

Participants in these workshops find a safe forum for expressing needs, venting frustrations, and learning real, viable solutions for minimizing the stressors. Primarily, stress management techniques are what we've already learned: clean eating, exercise, restorative sleep, meditation, relaxation, play, and spirituality/purpose and meaning.

Here is a simple formula to practice when you feel stressed. You will have greater success with this technique if you write out your responses.

1. Identify the cause of the stress/stressors;
2. Process the information about the stressor (e.g., identify and express your feelings); and then

3. Adjust your attitude, behavior, or situation toward a peaceful resolution (e.g., more exercise, or saying "The Serenity Prayer").

> *God grant me the serenity*
> *To accept the things I cannot change,*
> *The courage to change the things I can*
> *And the wisdom to know the difference*

"The Serenity prayer" from the Twelve Step Program

A vital component of stress management is resilience. "Taking things in stride" is another way to say this.

Taking things in stride means not sweating the small stuff and recognizing that it's all small stuff. Taking things in stride means living in the present moment and being resilient when things don't go your way.

A person who goes with the flow and takes things in stride is *not* a lackadaisical do-nothing who never accomplishes anything. In fact, one might argue that the more resilient you are, the *more* productive you'll be, because you won't get dragged down by life's frequent curve balls.

When you take things in stride, you don't get so hung up on every crisis that befalls you. You do not get sad and stressed out because you make a mistake, eat a candy bar, or do not complete something on your "To Do" list.

I have had to work long and hard on this one.

I have a tendency to become emotional every time I have to interact with a jerk, hear about the death or divorce of a friend, or have to call the plumber, again, for the same leaky valve. I get impatient with long lines, excessive heat, people who do not keep their word, and sexists. I do not like droughts, forest fires, floods, and wars. I cry when I read about beaten dogs, school shootings, victims of human trafficking, and incarcerated innocents. Reality can be harsh, life is hard, people can be inconsiderate, and pain is abundant.

I read about people whose lives have been much harder than mine, who have figured out how to handle their stress. Soldiers who have been held hostage and tortured in war go on to become reputable political leaders. Young girls who have been raped in Afghanistan and Angola, grow up to become strong women who lead movements for social change. Victims of Post-Traumatic Stress Disorder (PTSD) learn to conquer this disorder through a disciplined practice of mindful meditation. Children with cancer teach us what it means to live one day at a time.

I was raised to do battle with adversity, to fight and compete for everything worth having. Occasionally, very occasionally, when I am in full balance, I do not become unglued by injustice or idiosyncratic behaviors.

I am still working on taking things in stride. I do better when I am balanced. For me, being balanced is eating and sleeping well, doing activities that have purpose and meaning, exercising, practicing Raja YOGA, meditating, and maintaining good relationships. To these, I must add occasional personal retreats and inspiring books that motivate me to stay centered and calm.

Developing resilience

"Whether you think you can or think you can't —you are right."

Henry Ford

In "Bounce Back" by Mandy Oaklander (*Time*, June 1, 2015), we learn that resilience is a skill set that can be learned. Resilience is neither genetic nor the result of family values. You don't need to be born with a mellow gene or raised by a mellow mama. We are all capable of learning this vital trait.

Key practices for enhancing resilience are mindfulness and meditation. Learning these skills is a key emphasis of the *Mindfulness-Based Stress Reduction* (MBSR) programs. Jon Kabat-Zinn, MD, developed this intensive, eight-week program at the University of Massachusetts Medical Center in 1979. The National Center for Complementary and Alternative Medicine (under NIH), has given many grants to this program to research its effectiveness in promoting healing. "Completed studies found that pain-related drug utilization was decreased and activity levels and feelings of self-esteem increased for a majority of [MBSR] participants." *(Www.mindfulivingprograms.com)*

Other practices for increasing resilience include maintaining a positive outlook, taking cues from people who are resilient, confronting your fears, learning new things, exercising, and not dwelling on the past.

Chapter 25

HIT YOUR STRIDE

"My higher self is with me at all times."

Deepak Chopra

Hitting your stride is about being the best that you can be, doing the best that you can do, and living in integrity. Integrity means saying what you mean, meaning what you say, and doing what you say you are going to do.

In my lexicon, hitting your stride is not just about what you accomplish. It's about what you contribute. It's less about *what* you do than *who* you are.

When you hit your stride, you leave a legacy. You are a model for others. You have made the world a better place for having been in it. You have helped someone breathe a little easier. You have inspired. You need not be a leader, a martyr, brilliant, or rich. You just need to have contributed something meaningful that has lasting value for someone or something.

Wisdom

Wisdom is within. We all have the capability of maturing into whole, well, wise elders. Our willingness to step out of ego and into mindfulness can make us wise.

A way to achieve the insight, intuition, and discrimination of wisdom is to be present in every moment.

One simple exercise for moving toward present-centered wisdom is to set your watch or phone to go off every hour. Pause at these moments and pay attention to what is happening in this precious moment. Release, relax, observe. Step away from what is happening and view the circumstances of the moment from a witness consciousness. To witness is to observe yourself from the outside looking in, to detach from what's happening.

A good visualization for practicing this is "Observer Self" by Jacquelyn Small, MSSW, reprinted in a collection of meditations by Larry Moen called *Guided Imagery, Volume Three (United States Publishing, 1993)*. In this visualization, we are asked to think of an agitating situation, and then rise into the clouds and look down on what is really happening.

We often play witness with our friends without realizing it. We patiently listen to our friends' thankless complaining and endless loop of obsession and self-absorption. We listen, but under our breath, we're saying to ourselves, "Why is she getting so upset? This is really no big deal…"

If your friend could be taught to step outside herself, to pause, to breathe, she would be a much happier and healthier human being. The same goes for you. If you could pause in the middle of your angst, step outside yourself and observe what's going on from an egoless, detached perspective, you are likely to return to a calm, contented self. You may even laugh or smile at the preposterousness of your prior demeanor.

Self-confidence

"I'm selfish, impatient, and a little insecure.
I make mistakes, I am out of control, and at times hard to handle.
But if you can't handle me at my worst,
then you sure as hell don't deserve me at my best."

Marilyn Monroe

Self-confidence is the state of being certain of one's self, one's abilities. *(New Webster's Dictionary)*.

How we feel about ourselves is directly related to how we feel about others and the world around us.

Self-confidence is often related to how we were raised. The more positive our early experiences, the greater likelihood of our developing into a confident adult. Conversely, if our early experiences were filled with negativity and criticism, we may grow up to lack confidence.

The good news is that the more successes we have in life – in our personal and professional life - the more our self-confidence grows. There are also many techniques for building self-confidence. Not surprisingly, there is much overlap between building self-confidence and sustaining a wellness practice. Eat clean, move your body, do things which bring you joy, nourish your mind, step out of your comfort zone enough to like it, and trust your instincts.

Having doubts and making mistakes are part of human existence. As often as not, we can use these to move us forward instead of allowing them to pull us down.

Consider these techniques for building self-confidence:

1. Try a new direction. A new path awakens you.
2. Find your innate value; make your happiness based on your own self-worth.
3. Stop comparing yourself to others.
4. Be around people who make you feel good, and do not spend time with people who do not make you feel good.
5. Ask for help when you are overwhelmed.
6. Face your fears.
7. Notice when you *are* confident.
8. Choose to do what really matters to you.
9. Don't be a people-pleaser. Don't say yes to tasks just to be polite.
10. Use your strengths to overcome your weaknesses.
11. Be introspective about your mistakes, but don't beat yourself up.
12. Suspend second-guessing.
13. Give yourself a pat on the back for a recent accomplishment.

Who inspires you?

I believe that all of us have the *potential* to reach high levels of greatness, although not all of us get there. Will you be someone who inspires others? Do you think of yourself as someone people seek out for inspiration and motivation? Is this important to you?

Reading about and listening to charismatic leaders is a good way to keep you moving forward. Who are some of the people who have inspired you throughout your lifetime? Who inspires you now?

When Pope Francis visited America in September 2015, he brought members of Congress to their knees. For a moment, partisan differences faded into the reality of a greater truth. And so it was with citizens across the nation, regardless of creed or credo. For a few days, we stopped what we were doing and considered instead what we were *meant* to be doing.

Following are a few excerpts from his powerful presentation to Congress:

> *Our efforts must aim at restoring hope, righting wrongs, maintaining commitments, and thus promoting the well-being of individuals and of peoples. We must move forward together, as one, in a renewed spirit of fraternity and solidarity, cooperating generously for the common good.*

★★★

> *If politics must truly be at the service of the human person, it follows that it cannot be a slave to the economy and finance. Politics is, instead, an expression of our compelling need to live as one, in order to build as one the greatest common good: that of a community which*

sacrifices particular interests in order to share, in justice and peace, its goods, its interests, its social life.

★★★

... Let us treat others with the same passion and compassion with which we want to be treated. Let us seek for others the same possibilities which we seek for ourselves. Let us help others to grow, as we would like to be helped ourselves. In a word, if we want security, let us give security; if we want life, let us give life; if we want opportunities, let us provide opportunities. The yardstick we use for others will be the yardstick which time will use for us.

★★★

Now is the time for courageous actions and strategies, aimed at implementing a culture of care and an integrated approach to combating poverty, restoring dignity to the excluded, and at the same time protecting nature. We have the freedom needed to ... put technology at the service of another type of progress, one which is healthier, more human, more social, and more integral.

People Who Inspire Me
Distinguished Guests at My Dinner Party

List the names of ten people, living or dead, whom you admire for their wisdom and would like to gather for a dinner party in your honor. These are people you respect(ed) and admire(d.) This is an exercise for thinking about what and whom you value. [7]

1.

2.

3.

4.

5.

6.

7.

8.

9.

10.

Follow up Exercise:

What "qualifies" you to be in this group of distinguished guests?
List the characteristics you possess that distinguish you.

1.

2.

3.

4.

5.

Chapter 26

YOU CAN'T DO IT ALONE

"See the light in others, and treat them as if that is all you see."

Wayne Dyer

We are not an isolated species. Our natural preference is to live in groups or extended families and many cultures still do this.

This is not the case in America. Here, we emphasize the nuclear family. Nuclear families are not without benefit. They are influential in teaching healthy habits. Families establish patterns of "preventive care, exercise, hygiene, and responsibility, and they set the foundation for self-worth, resilience, and the ability to form healthy and caring relationships." *(James Martin, MD, Academy of Family Physicians)*.

For most of our lives, we live with a partner and our children— until they leave home. When the children grow up, we live alone. When we can't manage on our own, we are relegated to care facilities that may or may not be caring.

Low social support is linked to some health problems including depression, decreased immune function, and higher blood pressure.

Conversely, strong social support helps you live longer, build self-esteem, reduce stress, increase healthy behaviors, and improve mental and emotional health.

Having good social networks, healthy relationships, and a cooperative spirit are associated with societies where people live the longest. Other features that these societies have in common include:

- Eating whole foods and not eating refined sugar and processed foods
- Being active, especially in outdoor activities such as gardening
- Accessing affordable public health support
- Respecting and appreciating elders

The city where there are the healthiest active older adults is the coastal city of <u>Okinawa, Japan</u>. We find more centenarians in this small community than anywhere else in the world. Not only do they have the highest life expectancy in the world, but also they remain vigorous and healthy until the day they die, with few of the conditions associated with old age. Their good health and longevity are attributed to their collective gardening that they work well into their 80s or 90s, raising and eating nutritious foods they grow themselves. They are also a happy people with a strong sense of purpose and community.

In *The Blue Zones Solution; Eating and Living Like the World's Healthiest People* (April, 2015), author Dan Buettner invites us to copy the habits of the places where people live the longest.

This argument has merit. He calls these "Blue Zones." Besides Okinawa, other places where people live the longest are:

Sardinia, Italy

In the island city of Sardinia, many of the residents are also long-lived. The reason for their longevity may be genetic, but their Mediterranean diet, high activity level, positive attitude, and sense of humor also contribute to their long lives.

Loma Linda, California

The lone American city to make the list of people who live long and well into old age, Loma Linda is a community near Los Angeles with about 9,000 Seventh-Day Adventists. This religious group promotes vegetarianism and frowns on the use of alcohol and smoking. They also drink lots of water, exercise, and are not overweight. They value relationships, compassionate giving, and mental and spiritual health.

Nicoya, Costa Rica

Nicoyans have the lowest rates of cancer in Costa Rica. They sleep well, eat nutrient-dense foods, drink water that's high in calcium and magnesium, place a high priority on family and spirituality and spend significant time being active outdoors.

Ikaria, Greece

Chronic diseases are rare in this Greek island off the coast of Turkey. They have less cancer, heart disease, and dementia than their American counterparts. People have visited Ikaria for its enriching mineral hot springs for centuries. A social people, Ikarians are walkers, farmers, and fishers. They also enjoy a Mediterranean diet and love their afternoon naps! [8]

In a comical interview in *The New York Times,* August 2015, Dan Buettner debunks any dietary theory that is not consistent with what he has learned in these long-lived, healthy populations. But the real cornerstone of a healthy population, he tells us, is healthy relationships —people who purposefully look out for one another.

"The secret sauce is the right mix of friends," Buettner declares.

Chapter 27

HOW LONG WILL YOU LIVE?

My husband and I recently met with our financial planner to see how much longer we'd have to work before we could retire. A few questions had to be answered before she could crunch the numbers, most notably: HOW LONG DO YOU EXPECT TO LIVE?

I think I remember asking my grandmother this question when I was about seven and was severely reprimanded for my insensitivity. It is not the sort of question you are likely to ask your seatmate at a dinner party.

I am blessed with good genes from two parents who lived into their 90s. In the final weeks of my father's life, my oldest brother quizzed him on the name of my brother's high school teachers. My father remembered all their names.

Even though I have good genes and many friends, and I exercise regularly, meditate, drink ample water, do not smoke or drink much alcohol, I know I could do more to be healthier. How does one translate this knowledge of one's health and self-care, invariably tainted by subjectivity, into an answer to the question: How long will I live?

How long do I *want* to live? I only know that I want to die healthy. I don't want any chronic disease or debilitating medical intervention to take me out. I care less about *when* I leave this world than *how*. This is what motivates me to be active, to help friends do the same, to seek joy, to find purpose, to read, and to eat well 75% of the time. I want to be healthy, fit, and cogent till the day I die. I want to hit my stride and die at my peak. You, too, can share this goal.

Most of my clients are active, older adults like myself. We're old enough to start thinking about our mortality, but still young and motivated enough to do something about it.

It is never too late to initiate a wellness program. You can start where you are at any time. It is never too late to hit your stride.

<u>*Last Question:*</u>

What do you still need to do to hit your stride?

*List activities you need to pursue or practice for
becoming the best that you can be.*

1.

2.

3.

4.

5.

Chapter 28

HIGHER LEVEL WELLNESS

*"Here is a test to find whether your mission on
earth is finished: If you're alive it isn't."*

Richard Bach

Wellness is not just about your own self-care. It is about caring for yourself, for others, and the planet on which you live. Higher-level wellness embraces all of humanity and the whole earth.

All components of wellness are equally important and interdependent.

Eating whole foods will not guarantee good health if the food is not responsibly grown. Eating responsibly grown food is not enough to maintain good health if it is not accompanied by some form of movement. Moving because you think you should, and not in a way that gives you pleasure, will create stress. Stress may aggravate your ability to sleep well. Sleep is essential for optimal physical and mental health. Optimal physical and mental health also depends on playfulness and positive relationships. Positive relationships require you to tap into your inner wisdom, to speak truth, to practice integrity. Living in wisdom, truth, and integrity is living a life of purpose and meaning. When you live a life of purpose and meaning, you are living well.

We must also consider the effect of our every action on the next few generations. You can actively practice this concept with your food choices. Choose foods that will enable you to live a long, healthy life till the moment you die, and will also sustain the earth for your children's children. To consume all the world has to offer without regard to future generations is to live a shallow life of greed.

Love your neighbor as yourself. Generosity begins at home. We must be ever ready to help our loved ones, our friends, and our neighbors when they are in need. Set up walking dates with friends. Bring salads to those who are ill or injured. Visit widows. Be generous with hugs.

Once you have mastered your sleep cycle, consider those who are sleeping on the streets, in hospitals, in captivity. Perhaps you can help someone else rest a little easier.

When you **Eat** clean, **Sleep** well, **Seek** enlightenment, and hit your **Stride**, you will feel better about yourself and you will be more able to help others feel better about themselves. You will be more balanced and you will have more energy to give. You will exude joy and you will help make the world a better place in which to live.

*Wellness is the constant, conscious pursuit of
living life to its fullest potential.*

Lenny Evans

PART V

Q & A

Before I started this book, I sent a survey to over a dozen friends.

It said:

> *"After 30 years as a Wellness professional, I am finally writing a book on the subject. I know what I want to say, but I'd like to hear what you want to know. What do you want to know about Wellness? What would prompt you to buy this book?*

Many of the questions have already been answered, but a few have not. Here are the answers to a few stray questions.

Q: I'd like to know more about the medicinal effect of various foods.

Valarie

A: Most whole foods are beneficial. Most processed foods are not. My "Best Food Lists" include foods that have the greatest functional benefits.

Until they create an external hard drive that can be plugged directly into my brain, I choose to depend on the Internet for these details. I entered the keywords: "Medicinal Benefits of Foods" into my search engine. This is the first one to come up: *www.medicalnewstoday.com*

This site gives you the medical benefits of what they consider to be the top 10 foods and cites the studies that evidence these benefits. e.g., **Almonds** help prevent cardiovascular disease, cut the risk of cancer, and help prolong life. **Arugula,** along with other leafy greens, has been shown to lower blood pressure, reduce the amount of oxygen needed during exercise, enhance athletic performance, and prevent osteoporosis. **Asparagus** helps reduced the risk of diabetes, kidney stones, and neural tube defects in babies. That's just the "A's"…

Q: How do I maintain control, while dining out with friends?

Carol

A: Dining out is one of the biggest challenges for me. There are so many temptations at restaurants: cocktails, wine, breadbaskets, mashed potatoes, and desserts. It's hard to give them all up. Here are a few suggestions for approaching social events.

<u>You don't HAVE to dine out...</u>
When someone asks to meet me for lunch, I counter with an offer to go for a walk instead.

Invite them over for a home-cooked meal. Maybe they'll reciprocate with the same. Home cooking is healthier.

<u>Set Boundaries for yourself</u>

- Skip the breadbasket. I am now gluten-sensitive (but not celiac) so the breadbasket is off limits 99% of the time. It's when they serve it with dipping oil that I cave in. And I can't resist the homemade skillet cornbread from *Bandera's*. Demand a say in the dining location; suggest places other than those that serve temptations you cannot resist.
- Split entrées like you split desserts. Splitting desserts seems to have become common practice. Even when

you don't know your meal partners very well, most love the opportunity to have a teaspoon or two of the chocolate mousse. You can also do this with an entrée. Don't be afraid to ask. On the other hand, don't get stuck splitting something you don't really like or want.

• Decide ahead of time what kind and how much alcohol you will drink. One of my greatest frustrations is dining with people who order *another* bottle of wine without checking in. Make clear you are only good for one or two glasses. I don't drink too much wine anymore because it makes me sleepy. (I much prefer Tequila.)

Consider the *Weight Watchers*™ "Points" system©

At the meal, eat what you love, skip what you don't. I'd much rather have dessert than wine. Most people are the opposite.

You may also skip a meal or eat lightly on the day before or after an indulgent dining out experience. But do not starve yourself the day of an evening meal. If you go to the meal hungry you may consume the whole breadbasket and order too much food.

Q: How do I not let others make me feel bad when I say "no thank you" to dessert?

Ellen

A: This is the problem of a people pleaser who is valuing others' opinions over her own. Even if your whole book group teases you for not having a slice of pie when they are having one, it is their problem. Perhaps they are over-weight or under-loved, and their criticism of you comes from an unbalanced place. Stick to *your* truth. Value yourself. Do what's best for you, not for others. Say "No, thank you," smile, and let it go. In the long run, will they really think less of you for turning down a dessert?

Q: Evidence-based recommendations that review real research on wellness

Tom, MD

A: I'll level with you: I'm not sure all the information I have provided is evidence-based. I have used reputable sources (e.g. NIH, Harvard, Mayo Clinic, Johns Hopkins, WHO) but even they are fallible. Nutritional science is a highly volatile, ever-changing, contentious realm. Witness the fact that fats are back in favor and the USDA food pyramid is now out of favor.

Also, my target audience for this book is active older adults. I wrote this book for your *patients;* it was never my intention to write an academic review of evidence-based research. I leave that to the medical journals. Some of the most reputable journals for evidence-based wellness studies are: *Journal of Evidence-Based Complementary & Alternative Medicine* (JEBCAM,) https://us.sagepub.com; *Alternative and Complementary Therapies,www.liebertpub.com/act; Alternative Therapies in Health and Medicine,* www.alternative-therapies.com; *The Journal of Alternative and complementary Medicine, liebertpub.com/acm; Journal of Integrative Medicine, www.jcimjournal.com/jim.*

Q: How do I heal my lungs after years of smoking?

Linda Jo

A: If you do not have COPD and can still breathe, then breathe deeply. Can you do that?

I highly recommend breathing exercises. In YOGA, it is known as "Pranayama." This practice will help pump out toxins, improve respiration, and increase lung capacity. In Ayurvedic medicine, which is the medical companion to YOGA, Pranayama is said to raise the "Prana" or "Life Force" in your body.

To get started, just breathe deeply whenever you think about it. If you have asthma or bronchitis, breathing deeply may make you cough. That's okay. That's the gunk coming up. Spit it out. Keep at it.

There are many different breathing practices. Here are some to get you started:

1. Inhale deeply, exhale slowly (basic).
2. Inhale deeply to the count of 5, exhale slowly to the count of 5.
3. Inhale deeply to count of 5, hold for 5, exhale for 5. (Increase to higher numbers as you become proficient.)
4. Inhale and exhale through the nose.
5. Inhale through the nose, exhale through the mouth.
6. Roll your tongue or purse your lips as if you were to whistle, and inhale through the mouth, exhale through the nose.

Do a few of these three times a day – before you get out of bed and before you go to sleep and one more time during the day.

If you get light headed and dizzy, it means you are breathing out more than you are taking in. Make sure you get a big inhalation.

If you want more of these breathing exercises, contact me at theodora@wilnerweb.com

Q: Why do we need Vitamin D?

Ruth

A. This information is provided by the *National Institutes of Health, Office of Dietary Supplements*

Vitamin D is a fat-soluble vitamin that is in very few foods. It is obtained from sunlight, when UV rays strike the skin and trigger vitamin D synthesis. Because we are wearing more sunscreen to protect us from these same cancer-causing UV rays, more and more physicians have been urging the use of vitamin D supplements.

Vitamin D promotes calcium absorption in the gut. It is needed for bone growth. Vitamin D also assists with cell growth, immune function, and reduction of inflammation. Without sufficient Vitamin D, bones can become thin and brittle. Together with calcium, Vitamin D helps protect older adults from osteoporosis. Recent studies have also shown Vitamin D to be effective in supporting lung function and cardiovascular health and in diabetes management in regulating insulin levels.

Conservative recommended dietary allowances are 400 IU, 0-12 months old, 600IU, 1-70 years old, and 800IU for those over 70. Functional docs and natural healers will recommend 2-5000 IU of high quality Vitamin D3s. At your annual physical, ask your physician to check your Vitamin D levels.

Food sources of Vitamin D include the flesh of fatty fish (such as salmon, tuna, or mackerel). Small amounts are found in liver, cheese, and egg yolks. Most of the U.S. milk supply is fortified with a small amount of Vitamin D (100 IU Vitamin D per cup.)

Vitamin D deficiencies are usually the result of dietary inadequacy, impaired absorption, or increased excretion (say, from vigorous exercise).

Rickets and osteomalacia (weak bones) are the classical Vitamin D deficiency diseases. Rickets are characterized by a failure of the bone tissue to mineralize properly, resulting in soft bones and skeletal deformities. Insufficient Vitamin D contributes to osteoporosis (low bone mass and structural deterioration of bone tissue) that increases bone fragility.

Q: What are some natural ways — besides reducing salt— to reduce my high blood pressure?

Susan

A: High blood pressure, we know, is a risk factor for heart disease. Because of this, the heart association and heart clinics were amongst the first to advocate wellness practices that have been *proven* to lower high blood pressure. I'm sure you've heard these suggestions before, but listen again. Besides lowering your use of sodium (especially high in frozen foods,) please:

- Lose 10% of your body weight
- Exercise at least 30 minutes most days
- Eat clean (see *Best Food List for Heart Disease* in Chapter 9)
- Limit alcohol
- Stop smoking
- Manage stress
- Monitor your blood pressure regularly

Q: Tell people to avoid excessive sun exposure.

Tom

A: Thank you for reminding me about this important prevention practice. Skin cancer is caused by excessive sun exposure. Skin cancer is the most common and most preventable form of cancer.

The Environmental Working Group (EWG) tells us that half of Americans who live to 65 will be diagnosed with skin cancer, which has been proven to be linked to the unrelenting ultraviolet rays of our sun. Too much sunlight can also create oxidative stress (brown spots) and will cause your skin to wrinkle prematurely.

Ironically, these are the same rays that create Vitamin D. Liberalized use of sun screen to prevent the danger of excessive sun exposure is in part responsible for Vitamin D deficiency. This is why we are relying more on Vitamin D supplements.

Please follow the American Cancer Society's recommendation to *Slip! Slop! Slap! and Wrap!* Slip on a shirt, Slop on sunscreen, Slap on a hat, and Wrap on sunglasses

Q: What tools besides meditation and YOGA will help control the moods that undermine our health?

Jeannette

A. Thank you for giving me this opportunity to summarize this book.

In addition to meditation and yoga, you may want to:

- Eat whole, organic, responsibly-grown foods, savored slowly.
- Sleep well through most nights in order to recharge and restore.
- Find peace, purpose, and meaning in what you do.
- Face your shadow self, transcend your wounds.
- Practice the eight elements of a physical fitness program.
- Take things in stride, and
- Hit your stride.

For a quick summary of the action items suggested in this Wellness Guide, look at the Wellness Inventory in the Appendix, section viii. Check off YOGA and meditation and any other health-promoting activities you are doing for yourself. The items you have not checked are ones you may want to add to help you control your mood swings.

Also, you will want to identify areas in which you are specifically out of balance. I recommend two effective self-tests:

One is my Interactive Wellness Wheel in Chapter 1. Completing this self-test quarterly will give you a graphic depiction of areas that need work.

Just look for the spikes and tackle them. If you are not able to do these on your own, seek the services of a health coach.

A more comprehensive test is called "Clean Sweep." It is available from *www.betterme.org/cleansweep*. This assessment contains a checklist of 100 items grouped in four areas of your life: physical environment, well-being, money, and relationships. It is the most exhaustive self-test I have ever taken, and leaves you with very specific data on where you need to "restore and polish" your life.

Q: Tell me about the damaging effects of EMR (Electromagnetic Radiation) and protecting ourselves from Wi-Fi, smart meters, cell phones, and other high-frequency electromagnetic devices.

Ruth

A: When one of my daughters was eight, she developed an anxiety disorder (trichotillomania). We went to about 14 conventional medical and natural healing practitioners to try to find a solution. One of these practitioners — a highly regarded Ayurvedic physician — asked if she might have been exposed to electromagnetic "currents." Indeed, she was attending a school at the time where huge, overhead power lines bisected the campus.

Theodora Wilner

Today there are more than two billion cell phone users exposed every day to the dangers of electromagnetic radiation (EMR.) Government regulators and the cell phone industry refuse to admit that any danger exists from these invisible threats.

European studies, however, suggest that cell phone radiation contributes to brain dysfunction and tumors and DNA damage. EMR may also contribute to conditions such as autism, attention deficit disorder, neurodegenerative disease, headaches, and behavioral and psychological problems.

Modern technology is subjecting us to huge amounts of artificially generated electromagnetic fields. We have altered our electromagnetic background more than any other aspect of the environment. We deserve more credible, scientific information on the effects of this.

In the meantime, you would do well to keep EMRs at a reasonable distance and away from your head. Use ear buds for your cell phone, do not keep your phone on the night table by your head at night, and use broadband (wired) networks instead of WIFI when available.

For more info:

1. *Cell Phones; Invisible Hazards in the Wireless Age* by Dr. George Carlo and Martin Schram, 2002
2. www.naturalnews.com/034268 cordless phones_electromagnetic_radiation.html
3. www.wififacts.com

Q: I hear good and bad things about coffee. What's the truth?

Bruce

A: Coffee has many benefits *and* deficits, according to the Institute for Integrative Nutrition. ®

My husband drinks about seven cups a day. I drink less than seven cups every other week. Who do you think is at greater risk for caffeine-related problems?

I used to drink as much as my husband when my day job (like his, now) required sunrise to sunset attention. Shortly after I withdrew from that workplace, I vowed to kick my coffee habit and never go back. The withdrawal pains were so severe that I have kept my word; I never want to experience the weeklong headaches, jitters, sleepless nights, and fatigue that I endured when I severed my coffee addiction. Now I only drink coffee when we go out for brunch after our Saturday morning YOGA class or when I have slept poorly and need extra energy for a long drive or evening commitment.

Please be aware that caffeine is in other substances besides coffee, including "white" soda pops and "green" tea. Look carefully at ingredient lists of supplements, protein drinks, and other "health foods." Caffeine is likely to be in any beverage that gives you more energy.

Here are the *positive* effects of caffeine:

1. Improves concentration
2. Keeps you alert
3. Increases sense of well-being
4. Enhances athletic endurance
5. Depresses experience of pain
6. Inhibits cellular damage from free radicals
7. Relieves asthma attacks
8. May prevent Parkinson's and Alzheimer's

Here are some of the *negative* effects of caffeine:

1. Amplifies stress levels
2. Raises blood pressure, increasing risk of cardiovascular disease
3. Causes irritability, restlessness and agitation

4.   Inhibits the absorption of some nutrients

5.   Causes digestive distress

6.   Increases risk for urinary and prostate problems

7.   Dehydrates the body

8.   Accelerates aging

It's up to you....

Q: More on aging

Carol

A. My clients are mostly active older adults, like myself.

Most of the information in this book is especially relevant for people who have had brushes with their own mortality or have watched friends die prematurely. Active older adults have more motivation to make the changes necessary for prolonging their good health.

It is possible to die healthy. This is what most of us want. We are not afraid of dying. We are afraid of the pain and suffering that often accompanies it.

The best way to keep living a quality life until the last possible minute is to practice the healthy habits promoted in this book.

"The best thing about growing old is that you did not die young."
(Author unknown)

Q: Are you going to tell people to wash their hands?

Meryl

A: OK: Wash your hands.

According to the Center for Disease Control and Prevention (CDC), "keeping hands clean is one of the most important steps we can take to avoid getting sick and spreading germs to others." Germs from unwashed hands can get into foods, drinks, eyes, nose, mouth, handrails, and toys. Hand washing with soap and running water removes germs and helps prevent diarrhea and infections.

Q. How little can I do and give up and still be healthy?

Nancy

A: I love this question. Nancy is giving voice to what you have all been thinking under your breath while reading this book:

What a bore!
The hell with this!
I don't want to give up my ice cream, my chocolate chip cookies.
I like watching TV.
I hate exercising.
Pass me a beer.

We are not perfect. People who seem perfect really aren't. Young people who are fit, lean, healthy, and gorgeous will age right along with the rest of us. In fact, the more emphasis they have placed on their external beauty, the harder time they will have with aging.

We need to go easy on ourselves. Rest, pleasure, play, and supportive relationships are right up there with clean eating and moving your body in promoting good health. Of greatest importance is to have fun ("A Recreational Universe", Chapter 18) and to experience joy and happiness. Note that in the "Blue Zones," cities with the highest longevity rates (Chapter 22), few live a life of denial.

One of my favorite formulas for eating — and this may speak most directly to your question — is the 80/20 rule, which I've also seen interpreted as the 90/10 or 70/30 rule. You give yourself your own percentage of how well you want to eat most of the time vs. how much you wish to indulge. I'm probably much more in the 75/25 range, which is why I am still 12 pounds over my goal weight. It is a choice I have made.

For no comprehensible reason, some of you have been dealt some health challenges that may require you to be more attentive to your health habits than others. Or not. After a heart attack, as many people return to smoking, drinking, and poor eating as those who turn over a new leaf and engage in healthier habits.

It is said that former President Lyndon Johnson, after a long career of public service and significant achievement, decided he wanted to spend his final years just having a good time. He drank and smoked and ate whatever he "damn well pleased."

You don't have to be healthy. You don't have to live a long life. You are the master of your own fate. You can do whatever you want. The choice is always yours.

ENDNOTES

1   I borrowed from many sources in my creation of this Interactive Wellness Wheel including but not limited to Life's Odyssey by Human Solutions, Inc., and Circle of Life by Institute for Integrative Nutrition.®

2   The FDA has given the food industry three years to comply with this new ban, so some of these products may have cleaned up their act by the time you read this.

3   100% grass feed meat tends to be a little tougher than the marbled, fatty meat to which we have become accustomed. To appeal to American tastes, some humane farmers are adding a little grain to their animals' diet at the end. This gets complicated.

4   To find a good counselor or coach, ask friends. Use the Internet. More and more counselors and coaches have websites that thoroughly describe their philosophies, fees, and locations. I offer 45-minute free tele-consultations. Contact me at theodora@wilnerweb.com to get started.

5   Just in case I did not appear grateful, I wanted to acknowledge my father's strong belief in education and am grateful for his financing my betterment through college. Besides financing private secondary schools, he also underwrote four college and two graduate school educations for his children — most of these in the Ivy League!

6   There are many different types of YOGA. Ananda, Ashtanga, Bikram, Iyengar, and Vinyasa, Vin, are examples of classic YOGA practices originating in India which have a Spiritual Teacher or Guru at their helm. Then there are modern variations of yoga— Restorative, Chair, Pre-natal, Paddleboard, and aerial YOGA that make use of props. YOGA teachers may attend trainings from different traditions and will end up with their own hybridized style. This is why it is important to try many classes until you find the one that resonates with you.

7   I didn't want to influence you in your decision making, so I have buried my most admired people here in these endnotes: Margaret Mead, Eleanor Roosevelt, Maya Angelou, Oprah Winfrey, Nelson Mandela, the Dalai Lama, Jane Goodall, Mark Twain, Jimmy Carter, and Pope Francis.

8   The former Soviet State of Georgia and the Hunza Valley in Pakistan used to be on the longevity list, but researchers found there are no written records to prove ages, and many from these areas exaggerated their ages. In contrast, Okinawa has family registries dating back to the 1800s.

APPENDIX

ADDITIONAL RESOURCES

I. SUPPLEMENTS

I am uncomfortable with this topic.

We should not need supplements. We should be able to get all the nutrients we need from our foods. Food is our best medicine.

But we do not live in a perfect world and we do not always eat well.

Dr. Mark Hyman. A functional physician who wrote *The Blood Sugar Solution* and the *10-Day Detox Diet,* believes that the only people who do not need supplements are those who:

> "… eat wild fresh, organic, local, non-genetically modified food grown in virgin mineral and nutrient-rich soils that has not been transported across vast distances and stored for months before being eaten…"

Hyman believes supplements may be avoided if you:

> "… breathe only fresh unpolluted air, drink 32oz/ day of pure, clean water, sleep 7–8 hours a night, move your bodies every day, and are free from chronic stressors, exposure to environmental toxins, and are genetically perfect…"

I personally take supplements but I wish I didn't. I am not always sure that what I am taking is pure, safe, or effective. Many of my peers and providers have their pet products that they recommend, and I am a sucker for their inducements and rationales.

PBS' Frontline aired a program in January 2016 which exposed many horrors of the unregulated Supplement Industry. Scores of supplements were reviewed for health and safety and found to be wanting. Many supplements were analyzed and found to be lacking the ingredients represented on their label. The Food and Drug Administration which regulates pharmaceuticals for safety and effectiveness, is not required to regulate nutritional supplements.

In California, we are somewhat protected by the "California Safe Drinking and Toxic Information Act of 1986," Prop 65 is intended to protect Californian citizens from chemicals known to cause cancer, birth defects, or other reproductive harm.

Prop 65 requires the state to maintain and update a list of chemicals known to be toxic. You can access this list at: *oehha. ca.gov/prop65.html*

Over 30 years ago, I created the "Environmental Health Coalition" of San Diego to look at the environmental causes of cancer. Still active today, it's activities have led to the passage of one of the first Community Right-to know laws in the nations, the first ban on lead-contaminated candies, and the first bi-national toxic site clean-up.

At one of our early conferences, we featured a renowned physician/ researcher, Samuel S. Epstein, MD who had written a book called "The Politics of Cancer." I remember being aghast at his discussion of the many chemicals in our world. Even if we could know them all, he said, we cannot begin to know how they interact with each other. He was particularly worried about the numbers of chemicals in cosmetics. I see that he has since written a book on this subject called *Healthy Beauty; Your Guide to Ingredients to Avoid and Products You Can Trust.*

You can also get this information through the Environmental Working Group *(www.ewg.org).* For $5, you can get their *Quick Tips for Safer Cosmetics* shopping guide. This wallet card contains tips on how to read personal care product labels. You can also explore their *Skin Deep*™ database to learn about the safety of over 70,000 products.

Professional lines of supplements that are only available through medical professionals may also be better. Thorne®, Metagenics®, and Designs for Health® are examples of these professional lines.

Many holistic health practitioners use an applied kinesiology chiropractic technique (AK) called "manual muscle testing" (MMT) in which you can hold a supplement up to your body and tell if the product will strengthen or weaken you. Although this method is used often by reputable and licensed practitioners, I could not find any evidence-based studies that prove the validity of this method.

Follow your intuition. Do what you think is best for you. To thine own self be true.

Bottom Line?

My advice on supplements, cosmetics, and all medications is to use them judiciously. Know what you are buying. Read the ingredients. Research them. Buy better brands that have higher internal standards. Do not buy generic brands at discount stores.

II. MEDITATION TECHNIQUES FOR RECLAIMING YOUR BODY

Body Scan Meditation

Lie down. Breathe deeply and slowly, in and out through your nose.

Place your hands on your belly so you can feel your belly rising slowly on the in breath, lowering on the out breath.

Now you will scan your whole body, one part at a time. Should there be any disturbances — internal mind chatter, external noises, or physical sensations, just note them, and then let go. Bring your attention back to your breath. Allow for any pain or discomfort.

Start with your **right leg.**
Curl and arch your toes.
Inhale deeply as you move your attention from foot to calf, through knee to thigh.
Exhale slowly as you release the tension from your thigh, through knee, to calf, then foot.
Release, relax and observe.
Repeat.

Switch to your **left leg**
Repeat the sequence (at least twice) on the left leg.
Be sure to release, relax, and observe between each cycle.

Repeat this sequence with your **arms:**

Right hand – forearm – upper arm – shoulder.

Up and down two times.

Remember to breathe.

Be mindful of sensations.

Release, relax, and observe between each cycle.

Then the **left** hand- forearm – upper arm – shoulder.

Next – your **torso and head**

Belly —solar plexus — heart center — shoulders — neck— throat — face

Finally, notice your **whole body.**

Up and down.

Repeat this two to three times.

Now activate your "Witness Consciousness." You might imagine that you have detached from your body and are now floating above in the clouds, observing your body from above.

Observe yourself resting calmly. Breathe. What do you see? What do you feel? Accept whatever is.

Breathe until all sensations merge with your greater self.

Before you come back, mentally affirm: "I accept whatever is."

When you're ready, let yourself float back down into your body. What do you feel? How do you feel? Wiggle your fingers and toes, circle your ankles and wrists, and when you're ready, slowly open your eyes.

Progressive Relaxation

Progressive relaxation focuses on relaxing the muscles of your body.

With progressive relaxation, you systematically tense and release each muscle or muscle group from the tips of your toes to the top of your head. This action allows you to feel the difference between tense and relaxed muscles.

*This is **not** a good practice for people who are already tense and tight. If you feel discomfort or cramping when doing this exercise, it may not be for you.*

Find a comfortable position, sitting or lying down. I prefer lying down.

Breathe deeply and slowly, in and out through your nose, until you begin to feel relaxed and calm, and until your breathing is rhythmic and regular.

Alter your breath so you are breathing in slowly and deeply, hold your breath, and then let all your air out. The inhalation will be smooth; the exhalation will be loud and forceful, releasing tension.

Repeat this until your breathing is rhythmic and regular. This will be the breathing pattern that accompanies all of the following movements.

Now send your attention down to your **feet.** On the In breath, squeeze, tense, tighten, contract your feet. Hold the tension in your feet while you are holding your breath. Then release and relax your muscles on the Out breath.

Now the **calves.** Tense, tighten, on the In breath. Hold. Release and relax on the exhalation.

Now the **thighs.** Tense, tighten, on the In breath. Hold. Release and relax on the exhalation.

Notice how the legs are feeling loose and limp.

Tighten **all the muscles of your legs**. Tense the muscles further. Hold onto this tension. Squeeze the muscles harder, tighter... Continue to hold this tension. Release and relax on the exhalation.

Now move your attention to your **arms.** Tighten your fists, forearms, upper arms, shoulders. Hold, tight, squeeze. Then release. Let the arms release and relax completely.

In between each muscle group, return your attention to your breath. Let your breath become rhythmic and regular. Inhale relaxation, Exhale tension....

Now the **buttocks.**

Inhale- squeeze and tighten. Hold. Exhale- release and relax.

Now the **back.**

Inhale- squeeze and tighten. Hold. Exhale- release and relax.

Repeat this sequence with the:

Stomach

Trunk (chest and back)

Shoulders

Neck

Now move to your **Face.**

Scrunch your eyes, cheeks, and chin

Now take a moment to just release, relax, and observe. Note how relaxed you feel.

To close, kick your legs and shake your feet and hands to release any residual tension.

Luxuriate in the calmness you have brought to your body.

Rest. Breathe.

Before you come back to waking consciousness, mentally affirm: "I will retain this feeling of peace and serenity throughout my day (or night)."

When you are ready to come back to waking consciousness, wiggle your fingers and toes, circle your ankles and wrists, and slowly open your eyes.

III. THEODORA'S SEVEN-DAY KICKSTART CLEANSE

If you have been overeating, or are hooked on sugar, alcohol, or caffeine, you may want to launch your program of healthy living with a cleanse. A cleanse (sometimes called a "detox") is the first phase of a long-term program of healthy eating.

A cleanse will pull you out of your doldrums, rid your body of toxins, increase your energy, strengthen your immune system, help you think and communicate more clearly, and improve your overall sense of well-being.

In the first phase of a cleanse, we eliminate the foods that most provoke toxicity, weight gain, and addiction. You will not starve on my Seven-Day Kickstart Cleanse. The food plan consists of green smoothies or omelets for breakfast, a soup or salad for lunch, and a protein + green vegetable for dinner.

You will let yourself rest during the first day or two of this cleanse. Depending on how many toxins you have in your system, you may feel some discomfort or headache-y. Epsom Salt baths will hasten the release of toxins.

On day three, you begin a gentle exercise program. Walking outside is optimal as you gain the triple benefit of movement, deep breathing, and the spiritual stimulus of nature. Increase length, distance, and/or duration on subsequent days.

Sleep. Consider a warm bath, *Nighty Night* Tea, or light stretching before bedtime. Finish your last meal two hours before bed and disconnect from electronics, including TV, one hour before bedtime.

You'll want to be kind to yourself this week. Relax. Get a massage. Listen to music you love and do activities that bring you joy.

For more information, or to sign up for Theodora's Seven-Day Kickstart cleanse, contact *theodora@wilnerweb.com.*

IV. BOOKS THAT LIFT YOU UP; PROPOSED READING LIST

All books by Baba Ram Dass (Formerly Richard Alpert). His first classic *Be Here Now* (1978) was written sideways, in circles, and with a bunch of different fonts to help you get out of your linear mindset. His more recent *Still Here* (2000) shows how he has managed to embrace aging and change after he had a stroke.

The Power of Now or *A New Earth,* by Eckhart Tolle.
All you need to do is accept this moment fully. You are then at ease in the here and now, and at ease with yourself.

Loving What is: Four Questions That Can Change Your Life by Byron Katie.
The Work teaches you to identify and question the thoughts that cause all the suffering in the world. It's a way to understand what's hurting you and to address the cause of your problems with clarity.

The Four Agreements; A Practical Guide to Personal Freedom, by Don Miguel Ruiz.
This author's manifesto for right living: Be impeccable with your word. Don't take anything personally. Don't make assumptions. Always do your best.

My Stroke of Insight, by Judith Bolte Taylor.

A brain scientist documents all phases of a stroke, which becomes a blessing and a revelation. It teaches her the power and purpose of the right brain and the feelings of well-being that are often sidelined by the mind chatter of the left brain. It is an inspiring testimony that inner peace is accessible to anyone.

A Path with Heart, by Jack Kornfield.
Miracle of Mindfulness or *the Heart of The Buddha's Teaching,* by Thich Nhat Hanh
Start Where You Are, by Pema Chodron

Jack Kornfield, Thich Nhat Hanh, and Pema Chodron make Buddhist thought understandable for the Western mind. They combine Eastern wisdom with Western psychological principles and emphasize the power of mindfulness and compassion.

Autobiography of a Yogi, by Paramahansa Yogananda
This is a masterpiece of spiritual literature. For all its depth, it is full of gentle humor, lively stories, and common sense. I didn't realize it when I first read it about 20 years ago, but this is the book that launched my yoga practice and career. Although he died just a few years after I was born, I consider Paramahansa Yogananda to be my guru.

The Lost Gospel of the Earth; a Call for Renewing Nature Spirit and Politics, by Tom Hayden
Too often, those who are political have no spiritual awareness and those who are spiritual are defiantly apolitical. This surprising tome bridges those two realms by appealing to our

innate divinity and giving us a political guide for saving our mother earth.

> *"One person walks through a redwood forest and sees the hand of God at work; another walks through the same forest and sees only board-feet. Which viewpoint ultimately wins over the hearts, minds, and allegiance of our species will determine whether or not we survive."*
>
> *Mona Clee, Amazon reviewer*

20 Questions for Enlightened Living; Peace and Freedom through Jnana YOGA, by Julia Tindall
Julia Tindall teaches us principles and tools from an ancient YOGA practice to assist us in coping with modern challenges. With practices such as "Witness Consciousness" and "Self-Inquiry," we learn to let go of limiting belief system and induce a more enlightened state of being.

Peace, Love, and Healing by Bernie Siegel, MD
An old classic (1998,) this book presented the idea that we have an innate ability to heal ourselves. This "revolutionary" concept for its day, has now been proven by numerous scientific studies. Even mainstream medicine now accepts the connection between our minds and our bodies.

V. VEGETARIANISM

Vegetarians avoid meat for many reasons. For some their meat abstinence is motivated by health. For others, it is because of their religious views, their concern for animals, or their commitment to using our earth more responsibly.

Our year-round availability of fresh crops, and the growing influence of cultures with plant based diets, have led to an increase in the number of people eating vegetarian diets.

Research on vegetarianism used to focus on its nutritional limitations, but recently, studies are confirming its health benefits and positive effect in reducing the risk of many chronic diseases.

If you plug the words "Vegetarian Diet" into the search window of the National Institutes of Health (_www.nih.gov_), you will find a 26-page listing of the studies that have been done on vegetarian diets.

For decades, red and processed meats have been linked to cardiovascular disease, obesity, and cancer. The WHO study of October 2015 reports that one hot dog or about 6 pieces of bacon a day will raise the risk of colorectal cancer by 18% (to an overall increased risk of 6%.)

In 2013, in a study of 70,000 people, researchers from Loma Linda University reported that vegetarians lived longer than meat-eaters. Researchers found that vegetarians had a 12% lower risk of death compared to non-vegetarians.

This study posed these reasons why vegetarians outlived meat-lovers:

- Lower blood pressure
- Less chance of heart disease
- Lower risk of cancer
- Lower risk of diabetes
- Less likely to be overweight

Types of Vegetarians

Vegans — Do not eat meat, poultry, fish or any products derived from animals, including eggs, dairy products, and gelatin

Lacto-Ovo Vegetarians — Do not eat meat, poultry or fish, but do eat eggs and dairy products.

Lacto Vegetarians eat dairy products, but no eggs

Ovo vegetarians eat eggs, but no dairy products.

VI. COUNTERPOINT: OMNIVOROUS DIETS

A friend of mine who strongly believes in a diet based on traditional foods, created the attached bibliography.

Claudia Ayers is one of my oldest friends. The coincidences that bond us are uncanny.

We graduated from the same class at Woodrow Wilson High School in Washington, DC. Almost 20 years later, we found ourselves in the same neighborhood in Sacramento, California. Each of us has two daughters who are about the same age. They attended the same schools. When we moved to Fair Oaks, a suburb of Sacramento, we moved to the same street where her ex-husband had also relocated with his new wife; we are in the same neighborhood book group.

Claudia now lives in Santa Cruz, in a sustainable "compound" of her own creation. It features an organic vegetable "farm" with a fruit orchard and free-roaming chickens. When we visited her recently, we were treated to the most delectable breakfast of fresh-picked vegetables sautéed in real butter, topped with just-collected sunnyside-up eggs, and accompanied by the best bacon I've ever tasted from a humanely-raised pig she bought from a nearby friend.

Claudia reads more in a week than I read in a month. A retired teacher, she spends much of her free time reading about nutrition and other causes close to her heart, and then becomes a rabid believer and promoter of that issue. The following bibliography is the outcome of her commitment to traditional diets.

Books *on*
Healthy Omnivorous Nutrient-Dense Diets
By Claudia Ayers

Deep Nutrition: *Why Your Genes Need Traditional Food,* by Catherine Shanahan, MD, & Luke Shanahan, 2009.

Dr. Cate and Mr. Shanahan present astonishing, even jaw-dropping, research on every page. This was my gateway to better understanding all aspects of health and the genetic implications of malnourishment. This book was especially written for people who want to become parents; but all grandparents should also own it and read it.

Primal Body--Primal Mind: Empower Your Total Health the Way Evolution Intended, by Nora Gedgaudas, CNS, 2009.

To have a healthy mind and mental outlook, you must also have a fully nourished body. Nora connects so many dots in this masterful and eye-opening book. The book should be an active reference book for all parents.

Death by Food Pyramid: How Shoddy Science, Sketchy Politics and Shady Special Interests Ruined Your Health.... and How to Reclaim It! by Denise Minger, 2014

Denise survived her own raw vegan days and did the hard work of reclaiming her own health by researching how various diets affect health and why Americans got so much bad advice about that to eat. Her key advice is that each one of us has a specific diet that is best for ourselves and that it is our job to figure it out.

The Big Fat Surprise; Why Butter, Meat and Cheese Belong in a Healthy Diet, by Nina Teicholz, 2014.

This is the latest in brilliant books about the importance of nutrient-dense foods and saturated fats. This book also tells the story about how we got it so wrong when the U.S. government began advocating low-fat and lean diets. Nina took nine years to research this book, following an investigation on the dangers of trans fats for an article for *Gourmet Magazine*. Ego, bias and premature institutional consensus misrepresented "scientific research."

The Whole Soy Story, by Kaayla T. Daniel, PhD, CCN, New Trends Publishing 2005. Soybeans are good for soil enrichment cover crops, but have far more drawbacks than benefits as food sources.

Grain Brain: The Surprising Truth About Wheat, Carbs, and Sugar – Your Brain's Silent Killers, by David Perlmutter, MD, 2013.

Wheat Belly, by William Davis, MD, Rodale, and 2011.
Mini review: Today's wheat is not like yesterday's.

Cereal Killer, by Allan Watson, Diet Heart Publishing, 2008.
Mini review: Cereals slowly kill us.

Sugar Blues, by William Dufty, Warner Books, 1975.
Mini review: An oldie, but goodie! Sugar kills us faster.

Why We Get Fat: And What to Do About It, by Gary Taubes, 2010.
Mini review: High quality fats are fabulous foods.

The Vegetarian Myth: Food, Justice, and Sustainability, by Lierre Keith, Flashpoint Press, 2009. Brilliant!

Animal, Vegetable, Miracle: A Year of Food Life, by Barbara Kingsolver, 2007. As wonderful as her novels.

Cure Tooth Decay, by Ramiel Nagel, CreateSpace, 2008. Tooth decay IS reversible! A big advocate of bone-broth.

The Yoga of Eating: Transcending Diets and Dogma to Nourish the Natural Self, by Charles Eisenstein, 2003.

Performance Without Pain: A Step-by-Step Nutritional Program for Healing Pain, Inflammation and Chronic Ailments in Musicians, Athletes, Dancers... and Everyone Else, by Kathryne Pirtle, 2006.

Nourishing Tradition: The Cookbook that Challenges Politically Correct Nutrition and the Diet Dictocrats, by Sally Fallon, with Mary Enig, PhD, New Trends Publishing, 1999. This is the nutrient-dense food eater's bible.

VII. COMPROMISE: "PEGANS"

I am a Pegan. Mark Hyman, MD, coined this term.

"Vegan diets studies show they help with weight loss, reverse diabetes, and lower cholesterol." Dr Hyman says. "Paleo diets seem to do the same thing."

Dr. Hyman goes on to examine the commonalities between these two extremes, and these become recommendations that I follow and on which many will agree:

- Eat a "Low Glycemic Load" – foods that are low in sugar
- Eat a variety of vegetables & fruits.
- Avoid foods with pesticides, antibiotics, and hormones
- Avoid chemicals, additives, preservatives, dyes, and artificial sweeteners.
- Eat a diet higher in good quality fats including Omega 3 fats, olive oil, nuts, seeds, and avocados.
- Eat organic, local, and fresh foods.
- Avoid processed foods
- If animal products are consumed, they should be sustainably raised and 100% grass fed.
- If eating fish, choose low mercury and low toxin-containing fish such as sardines, herrings, anchovies, and other small fish.

VIII. A WELLNESS INVENTORY

Check off the wellness activities you have completed today.
Do this for one week or more.
To keep current with these practices,
complete the log on your birthday and on New Year's Day

Check (✓)	Wellness Descriptor
	Ate whole, organic, responsibly-grown foods, savored slowly
	Ate leafy greens at every meal
	Moved my body
	Aerobic (increase your heart rate)
	Flexibility (stretch, tone, & balance (e.g., YOGA)
	Endurance & stamina (e.g., hiking, skiing)
	Strength (weight training, isometrics, YOGA)
	Practiced 8 components of optimal physical fitness: Bend, balance, push, pull, stride, squat, lunge, and twist
	Slept well
	Meditated
	Did something with purpose & meaning (e.g., spiritual practice)
	Practiced a random act of kindness or service
	Played or did something pleasurable
	Visited with friends or family
	Took things in stride
	Demonstrated Resilience
	Hit my stride
	Exhibited Wisdom
	Demonstrated Self-Confidence
	Drank a lot of clean water
	Other:

ABOUT THE AUTHOR

An Ivy League graduate and early Wellness pioneer, Theodora Wilner, MA, HC, RYT, has been a Wellness Advisor for almost 30 years.

Wilner offers presentations and workshops on Wellness, Stress Management, Fighting Fatigue, Clean Eating & Cravings, Second Half of Life, Enlightened Living, and YOGA.

As a certified health coach, Wilner helps clients find greater balance in their lives through clean eating, physical activity, supportive relationships, creativity, financial fitness, passionate work, spirituality, purpose and meaning.

She also teaches Hatha and Jnana YOGA

Theodora Wilner was born in Washington DC and lives with her husband of 32 years in Sacramento, California. She has two grown daughters.

www.wilnerweb.com

Printed in the United States
By Bookmasters